Write things worth reading. Do things worth writing about.

D1173719

雅思写作常考话题
高频短语速查手册

慎小嶷 / 编著　　**剑12版**

机械工业出版社
CHINA MACHINE PRESS

这本手册里面的 natural phrases 均取自 the Cambridge IELTS series, The Official Cambridge Guide to IELTS (OG), The Economist, The Guardian, The Telegraph, Daily Mail, Financial Times, National Geographic, Nature 等英美主流出版物,绝无"夹生"的中式英语,敬请放心使用。

Part 1 帮助备考时间紧迫的同学复习 Day 7 的 "120 急救短语"和扩展短语

Part 2 供您在考前练笔时开阔思路,或者在完成每一篇习作之后润色语言时查阅使用

Part 3 帮助已经进入考前倒计时的同学快速复习 Task 1 小作文的实用短语

多数官方高分议论文的长度是落在 260 words ～300 words 这个区间里面。对于这样的 short essay 来说,如果刻意追求语言"处处惊艳",反而会导致"口味过重"的不良后果。对于基础一般的同学来说,全文能用出 4～6 条 good phrases 就已经挺好了,多数用词都可以很平实,同时注意控制住语法错误(cf. 《作业本》Day 3)。

您还可以用《作业本》Day 8 里面的
近三年真题做思考练习

目　录

Part 1

120 <u>急救短语</u> 和扩展短语

120 Essential Phrases for the Task-2 Essay

Building blocks are important because they can encourage imagination and creativity.

—Pat

索 引

时间紧的同学请先把每一类里各编号后面的主词条（120 急救短语）记准、记熟。对考场实战来说，记忆的准确度和熟练度比记忆的数量更重要。

技能类短语

(包含学生、毕业生、儿童、员工的技能)

1 develop their skills
发展他们的技能

提示:

下面是一些和它有关的扩展短语,您可以根据自己的考前实际时间安排选择记忆,不必都记

- thinking and learning skills   思考和学习的能力

- reading and writing skills   读写技能

- foreign language skills   外语技能

- creative skills ★   创造力
   (请注意:地道英文里不写 creation skills ✗)

- artistic skills   艺术才能

- problem-solving skills ★   解决问题的能力

- computer skills   电脑技能,计算机技能

- social skills ★   进行社会交往的技能

- communication skills ★   沟通能力

- teamwork skills ★   团队合作能力

2 develop good learning habits
形成良好的学习习惯

- learn more efficiently   更高效地学习

- □ develop good eating habits　形成良好的饮食习惯
- □ develop good spending habits　形成良好的消费习惯
- □ develop good driving habits　形成良好的驾驶习惯

3 broaden their knowledge about ...
扩展他们关于……的知识

- □ get good grades / achieve good grades
  （学生）获得好成绩
- □ improve their academic skills
  提高他们的学术技能
- □ increase their knowledge about ...
  增加他们关于……的知识
- □ improve analytical skills　提高分析能力
- □ develop independent thinking skills
  发展独立思考的能力
- □ gain a better understanding of...
  （儿童、学生、游客等）加深对于……的理解

4 boost their brain development
促进（儿童的）大脑发育，例如：阅读，玩益智游戏
(educational games) 等

- □ encourage their imagination　激发他们的想象力
- □ make them more intelligent　让他们变得更聪明

5 **become more creative**

变得更有创造力

- □ think creatively　有创意地思考
- □ express their feelings creatively
  用有创意的方式表达自己的情感

6 **expand their horizons**

（旅行、学外语）开阔他们的视野、开阔他们的眼界

- □ broaden their knowledge and skills
  扩展他们的知识与技能
- □ broaden their interests　扩展他们的兴趣爱好
- □ take part in extra-curricular activities　参加课余活动

7 **improve their social skills**

提高他们的社会交往能力

- □ develop their teamwork skills
  发展他们的团队合作能力
- □ become more confident　变得更加自信
- □ encourage teamwork and sharing
  （教师、学校）鼓励团队合作与分享
- □ build self-confidence　树立自信

- □ **build** understanding and trust
  建立理解和相互信任
- □ **build** self-confidence　树立自信
- □ **build** strong family bonds　增进亲情

5

技　能

8 **work closely with...**

与同学（或者同事、队友等）紧密地合作

☐ take part in group discussions　参加集体讨论

☐ improve their teamwork skills
提高他们的团队合作能力

☐ effective teamwork　有效的团队合作（名词短语）

☐ cooperate with their classmates　与同学
（或者同事 colleagues，队友 teammates）合作

9 **increase their independence**

（活动、经历等）增强他们的独立性

☐ make them more independent　让他们变得更加独立

☐ improve their life skills　提高他们的生活技能

☐ time-management skills　发展他们管理时间的能力

☐ money-management skills　发展他们管理财务的能力

☐ prepare them for adult life
帮助他们为成年之后的人生做好准备

☐ manage their time well　★
（学生或员工）管理好自己的时间

☐ manage their money well　★
（消费者）管理好自己的财务

☐ manage their budget well
（消费者）管理好自己的开支预算

☐ achieve a work-life balance　★
（员工 employees）实现工作与生活之间的平衡

□ achieve a work-family balance
（家长们）实现工作与家庭之间的平衡

10 gain practical experience
获得实践经验

□ lack practical experience　缺少实践经验

11 prepare for employment
为就业做好准备

□ have more job opportunities　有更多的就业机会

□ vocational training　职业培训
（名词短语，请注意：vocational 前两个字母是 vo）

□ enter the job market　进入就业市场

□ compete fairly　公平地竞争

□ the knowledge-based economy
知识经济，以知识为主导的经济（名词短语）

□ career guidance　就业指导（名词短语）

□ improve their employability　增强他们的就业适应性

□ achieve career success　获取事业上的成功

> □ prepare them for the job market
> 帮助他们适应就业市场的需求
>
> □ prepare them for the future workforce
> 帮助他们满足未来对劳动力的要求
>
> □ prepare them for the knowledge-based economy
> 帮助他们适应以知识为主导的经济

技　能

12 **achieve their potential**

充分发挥出他们的潜力

- □ achieve their goals　实现他们的目标

- □ prepare them for adult life
  帮助他们为成年之后的人生做准备

- □ prepare them for later life
  帮助他们为将来的人生做准备

效率类短语
（包含学生、员工、生活、交通、媒体、经济的效率）

1 **save time and energy**

节省时间和精力

- □ make learning more efficient
  （新的科技）让学习变得更高效

- □ make shopping more efficient
  （网络商店）让购物变得更高效

- □ make communication more efficient
  （现代通讯工具）让沟通变得更高效

- □ work more efficiently　更高效地工作

- □ shop more efficiently　更高效地购物

- □ travel more efficiently　更高效地旅行

- □ communicate more efficiently　更高效地沟通与合作

2 increase their efficiency

提高他们的效率

- □ boost productivity 提高生产率

对比：

- □ reduce their efficiency 降低他们的效率

- □ boost productivity 提高生产率

- □ boost economic growth 促进经济的增长

- □ boost tourism ★ 促进旅游业的发展

- □ boost national pride ★
  提升公众的民族自豪感

---

3 reduce distractions

减少干扰

- □ cause distractions for … (students / employees / drivers)
  【反义】(对学生 / 员工 / 司机) 形成干扰

- □ concentrate on their studies
  专心学习 (study 的复数 studies 是指 "学业")

- □ concentrate on their work 专心工作

- □ concentrate on driving 专心开车

效率

4 **make the best use of their time**
更充分地利用他们的时间

对比：

□ is a waste of their time   是对他们时间的浪费（注意：这个短语里的 waste 前面习惯加 **a**）

5 **boost their performance**
提升他们的（工作或者学习）表现

□ increase their motivation
增强他们（工作或者学习）的动力

对比：

□ lack motivation   缺乏动力

□ feel bored and unmotivated
感到无聊而且缺乏动力

6 **make our lives more convenient**
让我们的生活变得更方便

□ make our lives more comfortable
让我们的生活更舒适

□ keep in touch with family and friends
与亲友保持联络

□ provide people with more choices
为人们提供更多的选择

□ inventions and innovations
发明和创新（名词短语）

□ scientific research　科学研究（名词短语）

□ labour-saving equipment
节约人力的设备（名词短语）

7 **find information quickly and easily**
快速、轻松地找到信息

□ search for information　搜索信息

□ make communication more efficient
让沟通变得更高效

□ make traffic more efficient　让交通变得更高效

□ improve public transport services　★
改善公共交通服务

□ control the number of cars on the road　★
控制路上行驶的汽车数量

□ reduce the volume of traffic　减少交通量

□ provide real-time traffic information to drivers
向司机们提供实时路况信息

□ upgrade the road system　升级道路系统

8 **influence people's opinions**
（广告、新闻节目、报纸等）影响人们的看法

□ inform people about new products
告知人们关于新产品的资讯

效　率

□ encourage people to buy things   鼓励人们购物

□ boost the sales of products   提升产品的销量

□ provide the latest news and information
   提供非常及时的新闻和资讯

□ inform people about important events
   告知人们关于重要事件的信息资讯

□ broaden people's knowledge and interests
   扩展人们的知识和兴趣

□ inform people about …
   是"告知人们关于……的资讯"

□ are influenced by trends   受到潮流和趋势的影响

□ have different tastes   ★   有不同的欣赏品味

□ have different incomes   ★   有不同的收入

□ have different budgets   有不同的预算

□ have different spending habits   有不同的消费习惯

□ are easily influenced by advertisements
   （儿童）很容易受到广告的影响

□ are easily influenced by violence in the media
   （青少年）很容易受到媒体里暴力内容的影响

□ are easily influenced by their peers
   （青少年）很容易受到同龄人的影响

---

9 make the country more competitive

让国家变得更具有竞争力

- □ contribute to the economy

  （旅游业、广告、历史建筑等）为经济做贡献

对比：

- □ make the country less competitive

  削弱国家的竞争力

- □ cause labour shortages

  （人口老龄化、低出生率）导致劳动力短缺

  - □ cause housing shortages   导致住房短缺

  - □ cause water shortages   导致水短缺

  - □ cause food shortages   导致食品短缺

权利类短语

（含自由、选择、机会平等）

1 have more freedom

（在家远程上班的员工、独居的人）有更多的自由

- □ give them more freedom   给他们更多的自由

- □ reduce their choices   尊重他们的选择

honor/respect

13

权利

- □ restrict their freedom　限制他们的自由
- □ reduce their freedom　减少他们的自由

2 should be a personal choice
应该纯属个人的选择

- □ a free and fair society　一个自由、公正的社会
- □ are forced to...　被迫去……

3 provide people with more choices
（科技、网络购物等）为人们提供更多的选择

- □ provide people with more food choices
  （食品科技）为人们提供更多的食品选择
- □ provide consumers with more shopping choices
  （网络商店）为消费者们提供更多的购物选择

4 can have more flexible schedules
（学生或者员工）可以有更灵活的时间安排

- □ can study at their own pace
  可以按照自己喜欢的进度学习
- □ traditional classrooms
  传统的教室（native speakers 也常用 physical classrooms "实体教室" 来指传统的教室）

- □ can have face-to-face discussions
  可以进行面对面的讨论

- □ develop good learning habits
  形成良好的学习习惯

- □ form close friendships with their class-mates
  与同学们形成亲密的友谊

- □ can achieve a work-life balance
  能够在工作和生活之间实现平衡

- □ can achieve a work-family balance
  能够在工作和家庭之间实现平衡

- □ spend more time with their family
  更多地和家人在一起

- □ save money on transport costs　节省交通费

- □ help to reduce traffic jams /
  help to reduce traffic congestion
  有助于减少交通堵塞

5 **have job security**
（员工）拥有工作的稳定性

- □ job satisfaction　工作满意度（名词短语）

- □ have a steady job　有一份稳定的工作

- □ have a steady source of income
  有一份稳定的收入来源

对比：

- □ have less job security　缺少工作的稳定性

15

权　利

6 are treated fairly

（学生们或者员工们）受到平等的对待

- □ have equal opportunities
  拥有平等的机会

- □ job applicants　求职者

- □ provide a friendly working environment
  提供一个友好的工作环境

对比：

- □ are treated unfairly　（某类人）受到不公正的对待

7 promote gender equality

促进性别平等，促进男女平等

- □ can choose subjects more freely
  （男生和女生）可以更自由地选课

- □ have equal educational oppor-tunities
  享有平等的受教育机会

- □ have equal opportunities for employment and
  promotion　享有平等的就业和升职机会

- □ share parenting responsibilities
  （父母双方）共同分担养育孩子的责任

对比：

- □ gender bias　性别偏见（名词短语）

- □ traditional gender roles　在传统观念里男性和女性各
  自应有的社会角色（名词短语）

- ensure equal opportunities for all students
  确保每个学生都获得公平的机会

- ensure equal opportunities for all applicants
  确保每个申请者都能获得公平的机会

- ensure fairness　确保公平

8 violate their privacy
侵犯他们的隐私

- security cameras　安全监控摄像头

- public places　公共场所

反义：

- respect their privacy　尊重他们的隐私

▌责任类短语
(包含家庭责任、学生责任、学校责任、社区成员责任、政府责任、媒体责任)

家长的责任

1 teach their children good behaviour
教给孩子良好的行为举止

- teach them the difference between right and wrong
  教孩子明辨是非

- role models　榜样

2 give them advice and support
给他们建议和支持

- respect their feelings　尊重他们的感受
- support their choices　支持他们的选择
- help them to achieve their potential
  帮助孩子充分发挥出自己的潜力
- build strong family bonds / strengthen family bonds
  增进亲情（bond 不是指007，而是指情感联系）
- share ideas and feelings　分享想法和感受
- solve problems together　合作解决问题
- share parenting responsibilities
  （父母双方）共同分担养育孩子的责任
- exercise together　一起锻炼身体
- take part in community activities together
  一起参加社区活动

对比：

- are not as close as they used to be
  不像他们以前那么亲密了

- family members　家庭成员
- team members　团队成员
- community members　社区成员
- useful members of society
  能创造有用价值的社会成员

---

3 **have busy careers**

有忙碌的事业

- □ have a busy lifestyle　生活忙忙碌碌

- □ spoil their children　溺爱他们的孩子

- □ cannot achieve a work-family balance
  不能实现工作和家庭之间的平衡

学生的责任

4 **achieve good grades / get good grades**

（学生）取得好成绩

- □ good behaviour　良好的行为（名词短语）

- □ become useful members of society
  成为能够创造有用价值的社会成员

- □ become responsible members of society
  成为有责任感的社会成员

对比：

- □ have behaviour problems　有行为问题

- □ do not follow school rules / break school rules
  不遵守学校的规定

- □ drop out of school　辍学

老人的责任

5 **elderly people**

老年人（名词短语）

责任

- look after their grandchildren

  (祖父母们 grandparents) 照看孙辈

- share their life experience with their grandchildren

  和孙辈分享他们的人生经验

对比:

- generation gap　代沟

- feel lonely and unhappy

  (老人们) 感到孤独而且不开心

- have traditional ideas about many things

  对很多事物持有保守的看法

- lead to misunderstanding　导致误解

学校的责任

6 **meet students' needs**

(学校) 满足学生们的需求

- help students to achieve their potential

  帮助学生们充分发挥出自己的潜力

- become useful members of society

  (学生) 成为能够创造有用价值的社会成员

- meet people's needs　满足人们的需求

- meet consumers' needs　满足消费者们的需求

- meet tourists' needs　满足游客们的需求

---

7 **provide a broad and balanced curriculum**
提供科目广泛、不偏科的课程安排

- □ core subjects 核心科目（名词短语）

- □ required subjects / compulsory subjects
  必修科目

- □ optional subjects 选修科目

- □ provide a well-rounded education
  提供可以促进学生全面发展的教育

8 **become useful members of society**
（学生）成为能够创造有用价值的社会成员

- □ become responsible members of society
  （学生）成为有责任感的社会成员

- □ compete fairly 公平地竞争

- □ provide a friendly learning environment
  （学校）提供一个友好的学习环境

- □ prepare them for employment
  帮助他们准备就业

- □ prepare them for later life
  帮助他们为今后的人生做准备

- □ prepare them for the knowledge-based economy
  帮助学生们适应知识经济的要求

责 任

社区成员的责任

9 do volunteer work / do voluntary work
做义工

- build good relationships with their neighbours
  和邻居们建立良好的关系

- make communities safer 让社区变得更安全

- help people in need 帮助贫困的人们

- take part in community activities 参加社区活动

- build a strong sense of community
  建立很强的社区感，增强社区的凝聚力

对比：

- harm communities
  破坏社区生活

- contribute to their community 为社区做贡献

- contribute to their country 为国家做贡献

- contribute to the economy
  （旅游业、广告业等）为经济做出贡献

政府的责任

10 improve public services
（政府）改进公共服务

- schools and universities 中小学与大学

- libraries and museums 图书馆和博物馆

- □ healthcare services　医疗服务
- □ public transport services　公共交通服务
- □ state pensions　由政府发放的公共养老金（名词短语）
- □ improve infrastructure　改善基础设施
- □ protect national security　保卫国家安全

11 create jobs ／ create employment opportunities
创造就业

- □ employ many people
  （旅游业、广告业、跨国公司等）雇佣大量的员工

对比：

- □ take jobs away from …　抢走……的就业机会
- □ cause unemployment　引发失业

12 reduce poverty
减少贫困现象

- □ low-income families　低收入家庭（名词短语）
- □ reduce social inequality　减少社会不公

- □ fulfil their family responsibilities
  履行他们的家庭责任

- □ fulfil their social responsibilities
  （个人或企业）履行他们的社会责任

- □ fulfil their environmental responsibilities
  （个人或企业）履行对于环境的责任

责 任

13 introduce laws to …

通过立法来……

- □ practical and fair （某项政策）切实可行而且公正的
- □ is a long-term solution 是长期有效的解决方法

对比：

- □ is impractical and unfair 是不可行而且也不公正的
- □ is a short-sighted policy 是一项短视的政策

> □ regulate violence on television
> 对电视上的暴力内容进行严格的监管
>
> □ regulate advertising aimed at children
> 对针对儿童的广告进行严格的监管
>
> □ regulate genetically modified food / regulate GM food 对转基因食品进行严格的监管

14 run campaigns to encourage people to …

（政府）举办大型的系列宣传活动以鼓励人们去……

> □ encourage people to exercise regularly
> 鼓励人们经常锻炼
>
> □ encourage people to have a healthy diet
> 鼓励人们保持健康的饮食结构
>
> □ encourage people to buy eco-friendly cars
> 鼓励人们购买环保型的汽车

15 compete fairly

（学生、运动员、求职者、企业）公平地竞争

☐ promote fair competition
  （政府）促进公平的竞争

媒体的责任

16 provide reliable information

（广告、报纸等）提供可靠的信息

☐ help consumers to make better decisions
  （广告）帮助消费者们做出更好的购物决定

☐ compete fairly　公平地竞争

反义：

☐ provide misleading information
  （广告、报纸等）提供有误导性的信息

对比：

☐ mislead the public
  误导公众

☐ reliable public transport services
  可靠的公共交通服务

☐ reliable healthcare services
  可靠的医疗服务

☐ a reliable source of energy
  一种可靠的能源

责　任

环境类短语

(包含环境污染、能源危机、转基因食品、动植物)

1 **damage the environment**

破坏环境

- □ create waste and pollution　产生垃圾废料和污染

- □ household waste　家庭生活垃圾（名词短语）

- □ industrial waste　工业废料（名词短语）

> - □ pollute the air　污染空气
>
> - □ pollute the environment　污染环境
>
> - □ pollute rivers and lakes　污染河流与湖泊

2 **create waste and pollution**

产生垃圾废料和污染

- □ cause smog and acid rain　导致雾霾和酸雨

- □ cause health problems　导致健康问题

对比：

- □ reduce industrial pollution　减少工业污染

3 **car fumes**

汽车尾气（名词短语）

- □ air pollution　空气污染

- traffic noise　交通噪声，也是交通污染的一种

- contribute to global warming　加剧全球变暖

- control the number of cars on the road　★
  控制路上行驶的汽车数量

- improve public transport services　★
  改进公共交通服务

- walk or cycle to work　★
  步行或者骑自行车上班

- encourage people to buy eco-friendly cars
  鼓励人们购买环保型的汽车

- develop cleaner energy　研发更清洁的能源

- eco-friendly cars　环保型汽车

- eco-friendly lifestyles　环保的生活方式

- eco-friendly tourism　不破坏生态的旅游业

- reduce people's dependence on cars
  减少人们对汽车的依赖

- reduce people's dependence on social
  networking websites
  减少人们对社交网站的依赖

- reduce their dependence on international aid
  减少(接受援助的国家) 对国际援助的依赖

环　境

4 rely too much on...

过度地依赖于 ……

- □ rely too much on cars 过度地依赖于汽车

- □ non-renewable energy sources 不可再生的能源

- □ rely too much on fossil fuels
  过度地依赖于化石燃料

对比：

- □ solar energy 太阳能

- □ wind energy 风能

- □ water power 水电

- □ does not pollute the environment 不污染环境

- □ renewable energy sources 可再生的能源

- □ depend on weather conditions 取决于天气的状况

5 contribute to global warming

(汽车、飞机等) 加剧全球变暖

- □ contribute to climate change
  加剧气候的变化

- □ increase greenhouse gas emissions
  (汽车、飞机等) 导致温室效应气体的排放量增加

对比：

- □ reduce greenhouse gas emissions
  减少温室效应气体的排放

6 put pressure on...

对……（自然资源、医疗体系等）构成压力

☐ grow rapidly　（人口）快速地增长

☐ meet consumers' needs　满足消费者们的需求

☐ the demand for consumer goods
对于消费品的需求（名词短语）

对比：

☐ use more natural resources
使用更多的自然资源

☐ create more waste and pollution
产生更多的垃圾废料和污染

> ☐ put pressure on natural resources
> （人口的增长、消费的增长等）对自然资源构成压力
>
> ☐ put pressure on infrastructure
> （人口的增长、旅游业）对基础设施构成压力
>
> ☐ put pressure on the healthcare system
> （人口老龄化）对医疗体系构成压力

7 meet their environmental responsibilities　/
fulfil their environmental responsibilities
（个人、公司、政府）履行对于环境的义务

☐ have eco-friendly lifestyles　坚持环保的生活方式

☐ reuse shopping bags　★　重复使用购物袋

☐ recycle cans and bottles　★　循环利用瓶瓶罐罐

☐ choose products with less plastic packaging
选择塑料外包装比较少的产品

☐ use public transport more often ★
更多地使用公共交通

☐ walk or cycle to work ★ 步行或骑自行车上班

☐ improve public transport services ★
改进公共交通服务

☐ introduce laws to protect the environment
通过立法来保护环境

☐ fine companies that pollute the environment ★
对污染环境的公司进行罚款（说明：这个 fine 是及物动词，罚款的意思）

☐ give financial support to research on clean energy
为清洁能源的研究提供资助

8 become overcrowded
（城市）变得过于拥挤

☐ urban residents / city dwellers 城市里的居民

☐ have more job opportunities 有更多的就业机会

☐ feel disconnected from nature
（城市里的居民）感觉自己的生活与大自然脱节

9 make... more attractive
让……（食品、城市、旅游景点等）更吸引人

☐ genetically modified food
转基因食品（按英美习惯也可以写成 GM food）

- ☐ GM crops　转基因的农作物

- ☐ grow faster　生长得更快

- ☐ increase crop yields　增加农作物的产量

对比：

- ☐ cause health problems　导致健康问题

- ☐ pose health risks to consumers
　对消费者们构成健康方面的风险

10 wildlife habitats
野生动植物的栖息地（名词短语）

- ☐ cut down forests　砍伐森林

- ☐ destroy wildlife habitats　破坏野生动植物的栖息地

- ☐ lead to natural disasters　导致自然灾害

- ☐ reduce biodiversity　减少生物的多样性

对比：

- ☐ protect wildlife habitats　保护野生动植物的栖息地

11 endangered animals
濒危动物（名词短语）

- ☐ wildlife products　用野生动植物制成的产品

- ☐ die out / become extinct　灭绝

对比：

- ☐ introduce laws to protect wild animals
　通过立法来保护野生动物

☐ wildlife reserves　野生动植物保护区（名词短语）

☐ create more wildlife reserves
创立更多的野生动植物保护区

12 animal experiment
动物实验（名词短语，"从事"动物实验动词搭配 do、
perform 或者 conduct 都地道）

☐ cause pain to them　给它们造成痛苦

☐ are kept in cages　被关在笼子里

☐ is cruel and inhumane　是残忍的而且不人道的

☐ is morally wrong　是不道德的

对比：

☐ medical research　医学研究（名词短语）

☐ develop new medicines　研发新的药物

☐ reduce their suffering　减少它们的痛苦

健康类短语

（包含健康的生活方式、老龄化、心理健康）

1 have a healthy lifestyle
保持健康的生活方式

☐ have an active lifestyle
泛指在生活当中经常运动、健身、从事户外活动等

□ do more physical activity
从事更多的体力活动

□ reduce the risk of heart disease and high blood pressure
减少患心脏病和高血压的风险

□ exercise regularly   经常锻炼身体

□ walk or cycle regularly   经常步行或者骑自行车

□ have a balanced diet   保持均衡的饮食结构

□ eat more fruit and vegetables
多吃蔬菜和水果（这个短语里的 fruit 习惯用单数）

□ achieve a work-life balance
实现工作与生活之间的平衡

2 cause health problems
导致健康问题

□ an unhealthy lifestyle
不健康的生活方式（名词短语）

□ have an unhealthy diet   饮食结构很不健康

□ damage their health   损害他们的健康

□ a sedentary lifestyle
缺乏运动的生活方式（名词短语）

□ are overweight
超重（overweight 的语气比 fat 要客气一点）

□ increase the risk of heart disease and high blood pressure   增加患心脏病和高血压的风险

健　康

- heart disease　心脏病

- high blood pressure　高血压

- diabetes　糖尿病

- obesity　肥胖症

- asthma　哮喘病

- lung cancer　肺癌

3 have a balanced diet

保持均衡的饮食结构

- home-cooked food　家里做的饭菜（名词短语）

- fresh food　新鲜的食品（名词短语）

- is more nutritious　是更有营养的

4 have a fast-paced lifestyle

（城市里的人们）过着快节奏的生活

- rely heavily on fast food　严重地依赖于快餐

- contain too much fat and sugar
  （快餐）含有过多的脂肪和糖

- frozen food　冷冻食品

- sugary drinks　含糖量很高的饮料，例如"烤鸭"们
  特别喜欢的 7 Up

- pose health risks to consumers
  对消费者们构成健康方面的风险

5 outdoor sports

户外运动（名词短语）

- [ ] increase strength, speed and balance ★
  提高力量、速度和平衡能力

- [ ] improve memory and concentration ★
  提高记忆力和注意力

- [ ] build self-confidence ★ 树立自信

- [ ] reduce stress and anxiety ★ 减轻压力和焦虑

- [ ] improve hand-eye coordination
  增强手和眼的协调能力

- [ ] take part in team sports / participate in team sports
  参加团队运动

- [ ] develop teamwork skills 发展团队合作能力

- [ ] give them a sense of achievement ★
  带给他们一种成就感

6 promote healthy lifestyles

（政府、媒体、学校）推广健康的生活方式

- [ ] raise people's health awareness 提高人们的健康意识

- [ ] improve public health 增进公众的健康

- [ ] encourage people to exercise regularly
  鼓励人们经常锻炼身体

- [ ] encourage people to make healthy food choices
  鼓励人们去选择健康的食品

健　康

□ **regulate fast food advertising**
对快餐广告进行严格的监管

7 **improve healthcare services**
改善医疗服务

□ **healthcare workers** 医疗工作者，例如：doctors 和 nurses（名词短语）

□ **medical technology** 医疗科技（名词短语）

□ **improve the healthcare system** 改善医疗体系

8 **population ageing**（英式拼写）/ **population aging**（美式拼写）
人口老龄化（名词短语）

□ **elderly people** 老年人（名词短语）

□ **retired people** 退休的老人（名词短语）

□ **rising life expectancy**
上升的人口预期寿命（名词短语）

□ **cause labour shortages** ★
（人口老龄化、低出生率）导致劳动力的短缺

□ **put pressure on the healthcare system** ★
对医疗体系构成压力

□ **increase the burden on taxpayers**
加重纳税人的负担

□ **save money for retirement** ★
（个人）为退休养老存钱

- □ raise the retirement age　（政府）提高法定退休年龄
- □ encourage immigration
  （政府）鼓励其他国家的人向本国移民

9 cause stress and anxiety
导致压力和焦虑

反义：

- □ reduce stress and anxiety　减少压力和焦虑
- □ cause health problems　导致健康问题
- □ damage their emotional health
  对他们的心理健康有害
- □ cause frustration　导致挫败感
- □ physical and emotional health　身心健康（名词短语）

10 have a stressful lifestyle
在生活中承受着很大的压力，"压力山大"

- □ have busy careers　有忙碌的事业
- □ work long hours　长时间地工作
- □ often work overtime　经常加班
- □ cannot achieve a work-life balance
  不能在工作与生活之间获得平衡
- □ work-related stress　和工作有关的压力（名词短语）
- □ are under great pressure with their studies
  在学业当中承受着很大的压力

- face tough competition for jobs
  （求职者）面对激烈的就业竞争

- face tough competition for promotion
  （员工）面对激烈的升职竞争

- face tough competition for business
  （企业）面对激烈的商业竞争

11 have a strong sense of belonging
（员工、居民）有很强的归属感

- lack a sense of belonging　缺乏归属感

- do not even know their neighbours
  甚至不认识他们的邻居

- feel lonely and unhappy　感到孤独而且很不开心

- build a strong sense of community
  建设很强的社区感

对比：

- lack a sense of community
  （生活在城市里的人们）缺乏社区感

- feel lonely and isolated　感到孤独而且很孤立

12 spend too much time online
用过多的时间上网

- spend too much time on the Internet
  用过多的时间上网

- spend too much time on social media
  在社交媒体（例如：Facebook 和 Instagram）上花费过多的时间

- spend too much time playing video games
  用过多的时间打游戏

- cause health problems　导致健康问题

- damage their eyesight　伤害他们的视力

- spend too much time in front of a computer screen
  在电脑屏幕前所花的时间过多，用电脑的时间过久

- spend too much time in front of a television screen
  在电视屏幕前所花的时间过多，看电视的时间过久

- rely too much on fast food　过度依赖于快餐

- rely too much on the Internet　过度依赖于网络

- rely too much on cars　过度依赖于汽车

- are addicted to junk food　对垃圾食品上瘾

- are addicted to social media　对社交媒体上瘾

健康

财务类短语

(包含个人财务、贫富差距、政府资金分配、国际贸易、国际援助)

1 develop good spending habits

形成良好的消费习惯

- manage their money well　管理好他们的财务
- save for the future　为将来储蓄
- manage their budget well　管理好他们的开支预算
- save for retirement　为退休养老存钱

对比:

- buy things on impulse　冲动地购物
- have high credit card debts
  拖欠很高的信用卡债务, 过着"负翁"生活

2 follow the latest trends

追随最新的时尚潮流

- consumer culture　崇尚消费的文化 (名词短语)
- create more jobs　创造更多的就业
- increase international trade　增加国际贸易
- increase the demand for consumer goods
  增加对于消费品的整体需求

- become selfish and greedy 变得自私而且贪婪

- earn more money 挣更多的钱
  (earn money 比 make money 更适合写作)

- focus on money and possessions
  集中精力于金钱和财产

- status symbols 身份和地位的象征（名词短语）

3 involve high costs
涉及到高昂的费用

反义：

- reduce costs 减少开支

- the cost of living 生活开支，生活成本（名词短语）

- high housing prices 高房价

- high transport costs 很高的交通费用

- high healthcare costs 高昂的医疗费用

- rising educational costs 上涨的教育费用

- rising childcare costs
  上涨的照看孩子的费用，例如：把孩子送到托儿所
  （nursery）或请临时看护人（babysitter）的费用

4 are more affordable
价格更合理

- low-cost flights 低价航班（名词短语）

- travel more efficiently 更高效地旅行

5 the gap between rich and poor

贫富差距 (名词短语)

- low-income families 低收入的家庭 (名词短语)

- live in poverty 生活在贫困中

- face financial difficulties 面临财务上的困难

对比：

- reduce the gap between rich and poor 减少贫富差距

- reduce income inequality 减少收入不平等现象

6 reduce costs

减少开支

- make large profits (公司、企业) 获得很高的利润

- are driven by profit
  (企业、广告等) 是受营利目的驱动的

7 give financial support to ...

(政府、大学、慈善组织、发达国家等) 为……提供资助

- receive financial support from ... 获得资助

- rely on governments for money (公共博物馆、公共图书馆、公立学校等) 依靠政府的资助

对比：

- reduce their dependence on...
  减少他们对于……的依赖

8 have more important concerns
（政府）还有其它更急需关注的问题

- only have limited funds　只有有限的资金

- improve public services　改善公共服务

- government spending　政府的开支（名词短语）

- give priority to ...　把……当成首要任务

> - is a waste of public money
>   是对公共资金的浪费
>
> - is a waste of time　是浪费时间
>
> - is a waste of energy　是浪费精力

9 improve people's standard of living
改善人民的生活水平

- are funded by ...　是由……资助的

- are under-funded
  （学校、医院、运动设施、博物馆等）资金不足

- face financial difficulties
  面临财务困难

10 is a waste of public money
是对于公共资金的浪费

- increase the burden on taxpayers
  增加纳税人的负担

财务

□ is an important source of government tax revenue
(旅游产业、广告产业、体育产业等)是政府税收的重要来源

> □ increase the burden on taxpayers
> 加重纳税人的负担
>
> □ increase the burden on the healthcare system
> 加重医疗体系的负担
>
> □ increase the burden on the state pension system
> 加重国家养老金体系的负担

> □ government tax revenue　政府的税收
>
> □ advertising revenue
> (媒体)来自广告费的收入
>
> □ admission revenue
> (博物馆)来自门票费的收入

11 contribute to the economy
为经济做贡献

□ contribute to the local economy　(旅游业、游客、移民、体育赛事等)为当地的经济做贡献

□ make the country more competitive
让国家变得更有竞争力

对比:

□ damage the economy　破坏经济的发展

□ make the country less competitive
削弱国家的竞争力

> □ attract many tourists
> （旅游景点）吸引大量的游客
>
> □ attract many visitors
> （博物馆、美术馆）吸引大量的参观者
>
> □ attract children's attention （垃圾食品的广告、
> 玩具的广告）吸引儿童们的注意力

12 employ many people
雇佣大量的员工

□ the tourism industry　旅游产业

□ contribute to the local economy　为当地的经济做贡献

□ create jobs for local people　为当地人创造就业

□ spend money on local goods and services
（游客们）消费当地的商品与服务

□ hotels and restaurants　酒店和餐馆

□ buy souvenirs　（游客们）购买旅行纪念品

对比：

□ create waste and pollution　产生垃圾废料和污染

□ put pressure on local infrastructure
对于当地的基础设施构成压力

财务

□ the advertising industry　广告产业

□ the art industry　艺术产业

□ the sports industry　体育运动产业

13 take away jobs from local people
抢走当地人的就业机会

□ long-distance food
被长距离运输的食品（名词短语）

□ provide consumers with more choices
给消费者们提供更多的选择

对比:

□ contribute to global warming　加剧全球变暖

□ take away jobs from local farmers and food producers
抢走当地农民和食品生产商的就业机会

□ increase greenhouse gas emissions
导致温室效应气体的排放量增多

□ contain harmful chemicals　含有害的化学物质

14 multinational companies /
multinational corporations
跨国公司（名词短语）

□ provide consumers with more choices
为消费者们提供更多的选择

- ☐ employ local people　雇佣当地的员工
　（说明：employ 是 employment 的动词形式）

对比：

- ☐ control the local market　控制当地的市场

- ☐ drive local companies out of business
　导致当地企业很难生存

- ☐ pollute the local environment　污染当地的环境

- ☐ have similar lifestyles
　（不同地区的人们）过着相似的生活

- ☐ are driven by profit
　（跨国公司）是受营利目的驱动的

- ☐ poor working conditions
　恶劣的工作条件（名词短语）

- ☐ threaten cultural diversity　威胁文化的多样性

15 international aid
国际援助（名词短语）

- ☐ financial aid　资金援助

- ☐ development aid　发展援助（为了改善受援国的教育、科技、基础设施、医疗等而提供的援助）

- ☐ build understanding and trust　建立理解与相互信任

- ☐ is a long-term solution
　（发展援助）是长期有效的解决方案

- ☐ donor countries　提供援助的国家，援助国

- ☐ recipient countries　接受援助的国家，受援国

- ☐ boost economic growth　促进经济的增长

财务

- □ are interconnected

  （国家之间，经济之间）是相互联系的

- □ reduce their dependence on international aid

  减少它们（受援国）对于国际援助的依赖

对比：

- □ is a waste of public money

  （一些人认为国际援助）是对公共资金的浪费

- □ misuse the aid （受援国的政府）滥用援助，misuse 是 use 的反义词 "滥用"

- □ influence the politics of other countries

  （利用国际援助）影响其他国家的政治

- □ lead to more corruption 导致更多的腐败

安全类短语

（包含犯罪率、改造罪犯、青少年犯罪、网络犯罪、交通安全、国家安全）

1 reduce crime rates

降低犯罪率

- □ prevent crime 预防犯罪

对比：

- □ commit crime 犯罪

- rising crime rates　上升的犯罪率

- violent crime　暴力犯罪

- deter criminals　震慑罪犯（震慑人）

- deter crime　震慑犯罪（震慑行为）

- deter dangerous driving　震慑危险驾驶的行为

---

2 reform criminals

改造罪犯

- prepare them for employment
  帮助他们为就业做准备
- provide them with vocational training
  为他们提供职业培训
  （注意：vocational 前两个字母是 vo）

- family support
  来自于家人的支持（名词短语）
- provide them with career guidance
  为他们提供就业指导
- have a steady source of income
  有一份稳定的收入来源

- become useful members of society
  成为可以创造有用价值的社会成员

对比：

- have a criminal record
  有犯罪记录（名词短语）

安　全

3 give them harsh punishments
给他们严厉的惩罚

- □ are sent to prison
  被关进监狱（注意：send 的过去分词是 sent）

- □ serve long sentences　长时间地服刑

- □ lose their freedom　失去自由

- □ become overcrowded　（监狱）变得过于拥挤

- □ lead to resentment　导致怨恨情绪

- □ are likely to re-offend　很可能会再次犯罪

4 address the root causes of crime
从根本上去解决犯罪问题

- □ create jobs　创造就业

- □ reduce poverty　减少贫困现象

- □ reduce social inequality　减少社会的不平等现象

- □ regulate violence in the media
  对媒体里的暴力内容进行严格的监管

5 threaten people's safety
威胁人们的安全（threaten 是动词，threat 是名词）

- □ increase people's fear of crime
  导致人们对于犯罪的恐惧感上升

- □ areas with high crime rates
  犯罪高发区（名词短语）

- ☐ make communities safer　让社区变得更安全
- ☐ install security cameras　安装监控摄像头
- ☐ increase police patrols　强化治安巡逻

6 violent images

（电视节目、电影、电子游戏里的）暴力的画面（名词短语）

- ☐ copy what they see in the media
  （儿童）模仿他们在媒体里看到的行为
- ☐ copy what they see in video games
  模仿他们在电子游戏里看到的行为
- ☐ develop anti-social behaviour　形成反社会行为
- ☐ drop out of school　辍学
- ☐ glorify violence　（媒体）美化暴力
- ☐ are frequently exposed to media violence
  （青少年）频繁地接触到媒体里面的暴力内容
- ☐ become aggressive　变得具有攻击性

7 Internet crime

网络犯罪（名词短语）

- ☐ computer hackers　电脑黑客（名词短语）
- ☐ spread computer viruses　传播计算机病毒
- ☐ steal personal information　盗取个人信息
- ☐ online fraud　网络诈骗（名词短语）

安全

□ steal username and password information
盗取用户名和密码信息

8 are likely to re-offend
很可能会再次犯罪，很可能会重犯

□ prevent crime   预防犯罪

□ prevent dangerous driving   预防危险的驾驶行为

□ pay fines   交罚金

□ install red light cameras   安装交通灯监控摄像头

□ install speed cameras   安装超速监控摄像头

□ deter dangerous driving   震慑危险的驾驶行为

9 involve high risks
涉及到很高的风险，例如：太空飞行 space flights、危险运动 dangerous sports

□ involve high costs   涉及高昂的费用

□ involve high risks   涉及很高的风险

□ involve many challenges   涉及很多的挑战

10 protect national security
保卫国家的安全

□ wars and conflicts   战争和冲突（名词短语）

□ military technology   军事科技（名词短语）

对比：

□ build understanding and trust   建立理解和相互信任

□ promote peace and understanding
  促进和平与理解

文化类短语
(包含传统文化、多元文化、国际文化交流、语言、老
建筑、艺术、企业文化)

1 protect their heritage
保护他们的文化传承

□ better understand their heritage
  更好地理解他们的文化传承

□ form an important part of their heritage
  构成他们的文化传承的一个重要部分 (form 作动词时是
  "构成" 的意思)

对比：

□ erode their cultural identity
  (全球化、外国文化等) 削弱他们的文化认同感

2 threaten traditional lifestyles
对传统的生活方式构成威胁

□ traditions and customs　传统和风俗 (名词短语)

□ traditional values　传统的价值观 (说明：value 的复
  数是 "价值观" 的意思)

□ pose a threat to traditional lifestyles
  对传统的生活方式构成威胁

3 are more open-minded
心态更开放，更愿意接受不同的事物

- a multi-cultural society
  一个多元文化的社会(名词短语)

- respect cultural differences   尊重文化差异

- can speak two or more languages
  会说两种或者更多的语言

- have more creative ideas   更有创意

- understand and appreciate cultural differences
  理解并且欣赏文化差异

- are more tolerant of cultural differences
  对待文化差异更加宽容

对比：

- have different values and lifestyles
  有不同的价值观和生活方式

- lead to misunderstanding   导致误解

4 build understanding and trust
建立理解和相互信任

- work closely with…   与……紧密地合作

- work closely together   一起紧密地合作

- promote international cooperation   促进国际合作

- transcend national borders
  (国际合作、环境问题等) 超出了国家之间的边界

- □ draw on other countries' experience
  借鉴其他国家的经验

5 threaten cultural diversity
威胁文化的多样性

- □ cultural globalisation　文化的全球化（名词短语）

- □ multinational companies / multinational corporations
  跨国公司（名词短语）

- □ international trade　国际贸易（名词短语）

- □ share the same fashions and brands
  分享相同的时尚和品牌

- □ watch the same films and television programmes
  看同样的电影和电视节目

- □ have similar lifestyles
  （不同国家的人们）过着很相似的生活

- □ multinational media companies
  跨国传媒公司（例如：Disney, Fox, Time Warner）

- □ satellite television　卫星电视（名词短语）

- □ spread their own culture　传播自己的文化

- □ weaken other cultures　削弱其它的文化

6 make communication easier
让沟通变得更容易

- □ a global language　一种全球通用的语言

- □ international business　国际商务

文 化

- international trade   国际贸易

- is widely used around the world
  在全世界范围内被广泛地使用

- international conferences   大型国际会议

对比：

- lead to misunderstanding   导致误解

- language barrier   交流过程中的语言障碍（"消除语言障碍"：remove the language barrier）

- the expansion of English   英语的扩张

- the expansion of the Internet   互联网的扩张

- the expansion of multinational companies
  跨国公司的扩张

---

7 feel isolated

（说小语种的人们）感到很孤立

- an endangered language   一种濒危的语言

- a minority language   小语种

- is only spoken by a small number of people
  只有很少的人说这种语言

对比：

- the dominant language   主流语言，"强势语言"

- have more job opportunities
  （说主流语言的人）有更多的就业机会

☐ have more entertainment choices
有更多的娱乐选择

8 **connect us to the past**
（历史建筑、传统音乐）帮助我们了解、感受过去

☐ introduce laws to protect historic buildings
（政府）通过立法来保护具有历史意义的建筑

☐ are an important part of our heritage
（历史建筑）是我们文化传承的一个重要部分

☐ historic sites　历史遗迹（名词短语）

☐ attract many tourists　吸引很多的游客

☐ contribute to the local economy　为当地的经济做贡献

☐ famous landmarks　著名的标志性建筑（名词短语）

☐ tourist attractions　旅游景点（名词短语）

☐ give character to a city　赋予一座城市鲜明的特色

☐ make cities more interesting and attractive
让城市更加有趣、更具有吸引力

对比：

☐ lack character　（现代建筑）缺乏鲜明的特色

9 **adapt old buildings to meet modern needs**
让老房子适应现代生活的需要

☐ make them safe　让它们变得安全

文化

☐ update the equipment　对设备进行更新

☐ renovate old buildings　对老房子进行翻新

☐ remodel old buildings　对老房子进行改造

对比：

☐ demolish old buildings　拆毁老房子

☐ expensive repairs and maintenance
昂贵的维修和保养（名词短语）

10 enrich the local culture
丰富当地的文化

☐ public art　公共艺术

☐ public places　公众场所

☐ bring art into people's everyday life
把艺术带入人们的日常生活里

☐ expand their horizons　开阔他们的眼界

☐ attract many tourists　吸引很多游客

☐ the art industry　艺术产业

☐ create jobs　创造就业

☐ contribute to the local economy
为当地的经济做贡献

☐ broaden their interests　扩展他们的兴趣爱好

☐ reduce stress and anxiety　减轻压力和焦虑

☐ make them more creative
让他们变得更有创造力

☐ express their feelings creatively
用有创意的形式来表达自己的情感

11 increase job satisfaction
提高员工的工作满意度

☐ are treated fairly　（员工们）受到公平的对待

☐ feel respected and valued　感觉受到了尊重和重视

☐ achieve a work-life balance
实现工作与生活之间的平衡

☐ achieve their potential　充分发挥出他们的潜力

☐ provide a friendly working environment
提供一个友好的工作环境

☐ build a positive corporate culture
建设积极的企业文化

☐ have equal opportunities for promotion and training
（员工们）拥有平等的升职和培训机会

☐ are rewarded for hard work
（员工们）辛勤的工作获得回报

☐ increase employees' loyalty to the company
提高员工们对于公司的忠诚度

文 化

乐趣类短语

(包含休闲活动、虚拟世界、学习与工作的乐趣、探索与发现)

1 fun and relaxing

有趣而且让人放松的（形容词短语）

- play video games　打电子游戏
- play mobile games　玩手机游戏
- browse the Internet　上网
- play outdoor sports　从事户外运动
- reduce stress and anxiety　减轻压力和焦虑
- educational games　益智游戏，例如：online maths games 和 online language games
- play team games　玩团队游戏
- satellite television　卫星电视
- provide a wide range of channels
  提供多种多样的频道

2 encourage imagination

（广告、游戏、电影）激发想象力

- make children more creative
  让儿童变得更有创造力的
- are fun and educational
  有趣而且很有知识性的，"寓教于乐的"

60

- develop imagination and creativity
  发展想象力和创造力

3 in a virtual world
在一个虚拟的世界里

- share ideas and opinions 分享想法和意见

- share interests and hobbies 分享兴趣和爱好

- share photos and videos 分享照片和视频

- make friends online 在网上交友

- interact with their friends online
  在网络上与朋友们交流互动

- social media / social networking websites 社交媒体，社交网站，例如 Facebook，Twitter，Instagram

- online community 网络社区

- take part in online discussions
  参加网络上的讨论

对比：

- rely too much on the Internet 过度地依赖互联网

- feel lonely in real life 在真实的生活里感到很孤独

- reduce face-to-face interaction 减少面对面的交流

- cause social isolation 导致脱离社会的生活方式

乐趣

- interact with their friends on the Internet
  在互联网上和朋友们交流互动

- interact with their classmates
  和他们的同学们交流互动

- interact with local people
  （游客）和当地的人们交流互动

4 an important source of information
（互联网、报纸、广告、新闻等）一种重要的信息来源

- find information quickly and easily
  快速、轻松地找到信息

- search engine　搜索引擎（名词短语）

- have access to more information
  可以获取更多的信息

- provide more entertainment choices
  提供更多的娱乐选择

5 online shopping
网络购物（名词短语）

- online shops　网络商店，"网店"

- provide people with more choices
  为人们提供更多的选择

- buy things at lower prices　以更低的价格购物

- save time and energy　节省时间和精力

☐ can easily compare prices　可以很轻松地比较价格

☐ save money on transport costs　节约交通费用

对比:

☐ traditional shops / physical shops
传统的商店,"实体店"

☐ try on clothes　试穿服装

☐ provide more interesting shopping experiences
提供更有趣的购物体验

6 make our lives easier
(手机、科技) 让我们的生活变得更轻松

☐ are thin and light　很薄而且很轻

☐ save space　节省空间

☐ are easy to carry and use　便于携带和使用

☐ make our lives more convenient
让我们的生活变得更加方便

☐ rely too much on technology　过度地依赖于科技

☐ cause health problems　导致健康问题

☐ reduce face-to-face interaction
减少面对面的沟通交流

7 keep in touch with family and friends
与亲友们保持联系

☐ mobile games　手机游戏,"手游"

乐　趣

- □ spend too much time playing mobile games
  用过多的时间玩手机游戏

- □ rely too much on mobile phones
  过度地依赖于手机

- □ can get help quickly in an emergency
  遇到紧急情况时可以迅速获得帮助

- □ mobile phone radiation　手机辐射（名词短语）

- □ pose health risks to users
  对使用者构成健康方面的风险

8 are fun and creative
（广告）很有趣而且很有创意的

- □ make products more attractive　让产品更有吸引力

- □ boost the sales of products　提升产品的销量

- □ advertising campaigns
  大规模的广告宣传活动（名词短语）

- □ have famous people in them / have celebrities in them
  （广告）有名人在里面出现

- □ inform people about new products
  告知人们关于新产品的资讯

- □ build consumer loyalty　建立消费者的品牌忠诚度

9 give them a sense of achievement
给他们一种成就感

- □ achieve their goals　实现他们的目标

□ achieve their potential　充分发挥出他们的潜力

□ compete fairly　公平地竞争

□ feel motivated　感觉很有动力，"动力十足"

□ hardworking and dedicated
　勤奋的、敬业的（形容词短语）

□ build self-confidence　树立自信

10 increase their motivation
增加他们（工作或者学习）的动力

□ feel respected and valued
　（员工或者学生）感觉受到了尊重和重视

□ feel rewarded　感觉自己做的事情很有回报

□ career path　事业的发展方向（名词短语）

□ choose career paths that really interest them
　选择让他们真正感兴趣的事业发展方向

11 feel bored and unmotivated
（学生、员工）感到无聊而且缺少动力

□ fall into a routine　陷入按部就班的常规里面

□ repetitive tasks　重复的、乏味的任务（名词短语）

12 explore the local culture
探索当地的文化

□ expand their horizons　开阔他们的眼界

□ interact with local people　与当地人交流互动

乐　趣

☐ better understand the local culture
更好地了解当地的文化

☐ respect the local culture　尊重当地的文化

☐ tourist attractions　泛指各种旅游景点

☐ cultural attractions　文化景点

☐ historical attractions　历史景点

☐ appreciate the local culture　欣赏当地的文化

☐ experience different traditions and customs
体验不同的传统与风俗

对比：

☐ lead to misunderstanding　导致误解

> ☐ explore space　探索太空
>
> ☐ explore other planets　探索其它的行星
>
> ☐ explore their own potential
> 探索他们自身的潜力

Part 2

针对 常考话题 的 28 类 加分短语

Topic-Specific Phrases for IELTS Essays

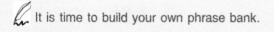 It is time to build your own phrase bank.

——Pat

IELTS 议论文 28 类
topic-specific phrases

索 引

議論文話題之 *1*

西方教育真正重视的技能和素质

1 gain knowledge about...

获取关于……的知识

告别中式英语

中国同学们在教育类作文里最爱用的"短语"之一就是 learn knowledge ✗，可惜它是典型的 Chinglish，因为在地道英语里 learn 和 knowledge 这两个单词不能搭配到一起，Pat 在北京的 native speakers 朋友们一说起中国孩子们写的 learn knowledge 就会 frown（皱眉头）

□ increase their knowledge about ...

增加他们关于……的知识

□ broaden their knowledge about...

扩展他们关于……的知识

□ deepen their knowledge about ...

深化他们关于……的知识

Test Tip：

动宾短语所特有的积极行动意味能够让论证读起来感觉更实际、不空洞，是帮助中国同学们避免论证空洞感的好方法获取知识当然重要，但从在英语国家开始上学的第一天起，你就会立刻感到：这里的学校对于 social skills（社会交往能力），life skills（生活技能）和 artistic skills（艺术才能）这三种技能的重视程度丝毫不亚于学校对于 academic skills（学术技能）的重视。中国同学们在思考教育类的论证理由时要特别注意不能忽视前面 3 个西方教育同样也很重视的方面。

2 develop their skills
发展他们的技能

□ improve their skills   增强他们的技能

□ boost their skills   提升他们的技能

在这些短语里还可以具体地写明是哪方面的技能，例如：social skills（社会交往技能），communication skills（沟通技能），life skills（生活技能），artistic skills（艺术才能）等

3 academic performance
学业表现

□ have good academic performance /
perform well academically   学业表现得很出色

□ get good grades / achieve good grades   学习成绩好

(1) 要写"提升"学生们的学业表现，动词可以用 improve 或者 boost

(2) 要写"降低"学生们的学业表现，动词可以用 lower (*v.t.*)

- □ improve their academic skills 增强他们的学术技能

- □ maths skills / mathematical skills 数学技能

- □ foreign language skills 外语技能

- □ reading and writing skills 读写技能

- □ computer skills 计算机技能

- □ analytical skills 分析技能

- □ communication skills 沟通技能

- □ problem-solving skills 解决问题的技能

- □ independent thinking skills 独立思考的技能

4 provide a broad and balanced curriculum / provide a well-rounded curriculum
（学校）提供可以促进学生全面发展的课程设置

curriculum 是对学校提供的各个科目的统称，也就是"课程设置"。一个具体的科目则叫作 a subject

- □ produce well-rounded individuals
  （学校）培养全面发展的人才

- □ meet students' needs 满足学生们的需求

  meet 在这里不是指遇见，而是指满足某类需求

- □ prepare them for employment 帮助他们准备就业

- □ prepare them for the job market
  帮助他们适应就业市场的需求

- □ become useful members of society
  （学生）成为能够产生有用价值的社会成员

□ should be added to the school curriculum
……应该被加入到学校的课程设置里

□ place more importance on... 更加重视……

□ have a wide range of interests and skills
拥有多种多样的兴趣和技能

5 an optional course
选修课程

□ a required course 必修课程

更难的写法是 a mandatory course 或者 a compulsory course

□ core subjects 核心科目

6 academic subjects
学术科目

□ theoretical knowledge 理论知识

□ concepts and principles 概念和原理

□ provide a foundation for developing practical skills
为发展实践的技能提供基础

□ the knowledge-based economy
以知识为主导的经济，"知识经济"

对比：

□ practical skills 实践技能

□ gain hands-on experience 获取实践经验

□ solve practical problems 解决实际的问题

□ apply and test their knowledge
应用和检验自己所学到的知识

7 develop good learning habits /
form good learning habits
形成良好的学习习惯

□ regular attendance   定时的出勤

□ pay attention in class   上课时认真听讲
（也可以写：pay attention to the teacher）

□ effective note-taking   有效的记录笔记（名词短语）

□ timely completion of homework
按时完成作业（名词短语）

8 achieve their goals
实现他们的目标

□ build self-confidence   树立自信

□ give them a sense of achievement
给他们一种成就感

□ increase their motivation to learn
增强他们的学习动力

9 reduce distractions
减少干扰

□ make them more attentive in class
增强学生们上课时的注意力
（attentive 是 attention 的形容词形式）

- □ concentrate on their studies 集中精力在学业上面
  (study 的复数 studies 经常表示"学业")
- □ cause distractions for them 对他们形成干扰

10 manage their time well
有效地管理他们的时间

- □ time-management skills 管理时间的技能
- □ make the best use of their time 充分地利用他们的时间

11 teaching method
(老师的) 教学方法

- □ make learning more efficient 让学习变得更高效
- □ learning style (学生的) 学习方式
- □ meet students' needs 适应学生们的需求

12 learn by rote
通过机械重复记忆来学习

- □ memorise facts and figures 记忆事实和数据
- □ multiplication table
  乘法表(英美口语里则经常直接说 times table)
- □ grammar rules 语法规则

对比:

- □ learn through experience 通过实践来学习
- □ learn through understanding 通过理解来学习

- boost their brain development　促进他们的智力发展

- scientific experiments　科学实验

13 think independently

（学生）独立地思考

- think creatively　（学生）有创意地思考

- encourage imagination and creativity
  （教师）激发学生的想象力和创造力

14 encourage students to explore ...

鼓励学生们去探索……

- explore areas that really interest them
  探索他们真正感兴趣的领域

- explore the world around them
  探索他们身边的世界

- explore a wide range of learning opportunities
  探索多种多样的学习机会

15 computer skills

计算机技能

- computer literacy
  对于电脑知识的基本了解（名词短语）

- computer proficiency
  对于电脑技能的熟练掌握（名词短语）

- educational software　教学软件

- □ have access to ...　可以使用某种资源

- □ become proficient in computer skills
  熟练地掌握电脑技能

- □ design and create websites　设计、创建网站

16 social skills
社会交往技能

- □ communication skills　沟通技能

- □ cooperation skills
  合作技能

- □ teamwork skills
  团队合作的技能

- □ team-building skills
  建设团队的技能

- □ develop into useful members of society
  （学生）成为能够创造价值的社会成员

- □ develop into responsible members of society
  （学生）成为有责任感的社会成员

17 take part in group discussions / participate in group discussions
参加小组讨论

- □ interact with their classmates　和同学们交流互动

- □ share ideas and opinions with their classmates
  与同学们分享想法和意见

18 team activities

团队活动

- team sports 团队运动

- team projects 团队课题（project 是指英美学校里极为常见的一种作业形式，projects 通常都会让学生们去积极查找资料并且进行研究）

- group presentations 集体演示

- improve their teamwork skills
  增强他们的团队合作技能

- encourage cooperation and sharing
  鼓励合作与分享

- work towards their common goals
  向着他们共同的目标努力

19 work closely with ...

与……密切合作

20 community activities

社区活动

- do volunteer work / do voluntary work 做义工

- develop their leadership skills
  发展他们的领导才能

- develop a strong sense of social responsibility
  形成很强的社会责任感

21 life skills

生活技能

- □ improve their life skills　提高他们的生活技能
- □ learn to manage their budget
  学会管理他们的消费预算
- □ financial skills / money-management skills　财务技能
- □ learn to manage their time well　学会管理好自己的时间
- □ time-management skills　时间管理技能
- □ sharpen their planning and organisational skills
  提升他们做计划和安排的能力
- □ can last into adulthood
  (某种习惯) 可以一直持续到成年之后

22 help them build self-confidence

帮助他们树立自信

- □ increase their independence　增强他们的独立性

对比:

- □ damage their self-confidence　打击他们的自信心

23 take part in sports

参加体育运动

- □ improve their balance and coordination
  增强他们的平衡和协调能力
- □ increase their strength, speed and endurance
  提高他们的力量、速度和耐力

- help them develop a positive attitude towards exercise
  帮助他们形成锻炼身体的积极心态

- encourage fair play and good sportsmanship
  促进公平竞争的意识和良好的运动员精神

- exercise regularly / take regular exercise
  经常锻炼身体（前者是英美通用的写法，后者则是英式英语里特有的写法）

- improve their health and well-being
  提高他们的身体健康水平和幸福感

- have a healthy lifestyle　遵循健康的生活方式

- eat a balanced diet　保持均衡的饮食结构

对比:

- damage their health　破坏他们的健康

24 promote healthy competition
促进良性的竞争

- respect others　尊重别人
- compete fairly　公平地竞争

25 extra-curricular activities / after-school activities
课余活动

- improve their social skills
  增进他们的社会交往能力

- ▫ develop their artistic skills　发展他们的艺术才能
- ▫ enrich their learning experience　丰富他们的学习经历
- ▫ expand their horizons　开阔他们的眼界
- ▫ broaden their interests　扩展他们的兴趣爱好

26 artistic skills
艺术技能

- ▫ drawing and painting skills　绘画技能
- ▫ performing skills　表演技能

  在英美的学校里面，drama club（戏剧社）和 school choir（学校合唱团）等很受欢迎

- ▫ understand and appreciate art　理解并且欣赏艺术
- ▫ express their ideas and feelings creatively
  用有创意的方式表达自己的想法和感受
- ▫ broaden their cultural interests
  扩展他们对于文化的兴趣爱好

27 stimulate students' creativity
激发学生们的创造力

- ▫ stimulate children's imagination　激发儿童的想象力
- ▫ boost their brain development　促进他们的智力发育

对比：

- ▫ limit students' creativity / stifle students' creativity
  压制学生们的创造力

28 achieve their potential /
reach their potential

充分地发挥出他们/她们的潜能

- □ achieve their academic potential
  充分发挥出他们的学术潜能

- □ achieve their artistic potential
  充分发挥出他们的艺术潜能

- □ achieve their athletic potential
  充分发挥出他们的运动潜能

29 prepare students for the job market /
prepare students for employment

帮助学生们为就业做好准备

- □ prepare them for the future workforce
  帮助他们达到未来对劳动力的要求

- □ increase their employability
  提高他们的就业适应度

- □ face tough competition for jobs
  面临激烈的求职竞争

- □ compete for jobs in a global market
  在全球化的就业市场上竞争

- □ job opportunities   就业机会

- □ career advice   关于职业规划的建议

- □ career path   事业的发展方向

- choose career paths that really interest them
  选择他们真正感兴趣的事业发展方向

30 job applicants
求职者

- academic qualifications　学历
- practical experience　实践经验
- personal qualities　个人素质

  在英美职场里，最受雇主重视的求职者个人素质包括：

  - honesty（诚实）
  - patience（耐心）
  - communication skills（沟通能力）
  - leadership skills（领导才能）
  - creativity（创造力）
  - a strong commitment to work
    （对于工作的强烈责任感）

- have more job opportunities　拥有更多的就业机会
- have better job prospects　拥有更良好的就业前景
- have a competitive edge　拥有竞争优势
- achieve success in their future careers / succeed in their future careers　在将来的事业当中获得成功

  【区分】succeed 是动词，success 是名词，只有分清它们你才能变得 successful（形容词）☺

教育里的机会平等

1 the rising cost of education
上升的教育费用

- tuition fees　学费

- living costs　生活费用

- low-income families　低收入的家庭

- face financial difficulties　遇到财务的困难

- need-based financial aid
  根据学生是否遇到财务困难来发放的资助

- merit-based financial aid
  根据学生是否优秀来发放的资助

- give financial support to...
  为……提供资助

- ensure equal opportunities for all students
  确保所有学生都能够获得平等的受教育机会

对比：

- are treated unfairly　受到不公正的待遇

- cannot achieve their potential
  无法充分发挥出他们的潜力

2 respect individual differences in the classroom
尊重学生之间的个体差异

  □ meet students' needs　满足学生们的需求

3 separate students according to their academic abilities
把学生们按学习能力分班

  □ achieve their academic potential
  充分地发挥出他们的学习潜力

  □ feel bored and unmotivated
  感到无聊而且缺少动力（unmotivated "缺少动力的"
  是 motivated "很有动力的" 反义词）

4 choose subjects more freely
更自由地选课

  □ gender bias　关于性别的偏见

  □ influence their course selection
  （某种偏见）影响学生们对课程的选择

  □ damage their self-confidence　打击他们的自信心

  对比：

  □ have equal chances to study what they want to
  （学生们）有平等的机会去学习他们／她们想学习的内容

  □ achieve their potential
  充分地发挥出他们／她们的潜力

5 cause stress and anxiety

导致压力和焦虑

- □ are under great pressure with their studies
  在学习当中承受着巨大的压力

- □ lose motivation
  失去动力

- □ make them frustrated
  让他们感到挫败感

- □ complain about …
  抱怨，"吐槽儿"

6 develop a sense of pride in their school

（学生们）形成对自己学校的荣誉感

- □ school rules　学校的规定

- □ dress code　关于着装的规定

- □ school uniforms　校服

- □ reduce distractions
  减少干扰

对比：

- □ reduce their individuality
  削弱他们的个性

- □ restrict their creativity
  限制他们的创造力

议论文话题 *3*

家庭对教育的作用

1 build strong family bonds /
strengthen family bonds

增进亲情（bonds 不是指007，而是指情感联系）

- have meals as a family　（家庭成员们）一起进餐

- do housework together　（家庭成员们）一起做家务

- share ideas and feelings　分享想法和感受

- solve problems together　通过合作解决问题

- participate in community activities together
  一起参加社区活动

- build a sense of belonging　建立起一种归属感

- achieve a good work-family balance
  实现工作和家庭之间的合理平衡

- help their children with homework
  （家长）帮助孩子做好功课

Pat's Note：

　　对中国家长来说这简直都不能算是个事儿，但在英美，这
却被视为好家长的标志。根据 BBC 去年的问卷调查，在英
国只有略多于 50% 的家长能够经常辅导孩子做功课

□ monitor their children's academic performance
监督他们孩子的学业表现

□ are more involved in their children's education
（家长）更积极地参与到孩子的教育当中

□ teach their children good manners
教给孩子良好的举止

□ help them develop a sense of responsibility
帮助他们形成责任感

对比：

□ are not as close as they used to be
（家长和孩子）不像他们过去那么亲密了

2 working parents
工作的家长们

□ have busy careers 事业很忙碌

□ spend their after-school hours without adult supervision
（孩子们）在放学之后的时间里缺少成年人看护

□ Internet addiction 网瘾

□ spend too much time online 花过多的时间上网

□ cause family conflict 引起家庭纠纷

□ high divorce rates 很高的离婚率

3 parenting style / child-rearing style
育儿方式

□ authoritarian parents 专制、强势的家长

家庭对教育的作用

▫ expect their children to do exactly what they are told
期待孩子完全按照被要求的那样去做

▫ stifle their creativity　压制孩子们的创造力

▫ damage their self-confidence　打击他们的自信心

对比：

▫ permissive parents　过于放纵孩子的家长

▫ spoil their children　溺爱孩子

▫ behave badly　（孩子）表现得不好，"不乖"

▫ behave as they please　（孩子）随心所欲地行事

正确的育儿方式：

▫ are understanding and supportive　理解并且支持孩子

▫ respect their feelings　尊重他们的感受

▫ support their choices　支持他们的选择

▫ respect their individuality　尊重他们的个性

▫ give them advice and support
为他们提供建议和支持
（注意：advice 和 support 都不能加 s）

▫ encourage them to think independently
鼓励他们去独立地思考

▫ help them build self-confidence
帮助他们树立自信

▫ help them achieve their potential
帮助他们发挥出自己的潜力

88

4 emotional health / emotional well-being

心理健康

> 【经济学人例句】This programme aims to promote emotional health among young people.

在真实的英美生活里，简洁的 emotional health 远比中国同学们熟悉的 psychological health 更常用

- provide them with emotional support
  （家长）为孩子提供心理与情感上的支持

- seek advice from their parents
  （孩子）向家长寻求建议

  对比：

- damage their emotional health
  对于他们的心理健康有害

5 develop good moral values

（学生）形成良好的道德观念

- teach children about social responsibility
  （家长或老师）让孩子们懂得自己的社会责任

- teach children the difference between right and wrong
  教孩子们明辨是非

6 good behaviour

良好的行为

- follow school rules　遵守学校的规定

- □ develop self-control
  发展自我约束力

- □ develop self-discipline
  发展自制力

- □ well-behaved students
  行为表现良好的学生

- □ teach them good manners
  教给他们良好的举止

- □ help them develop a sense of responsibility
  帮助他们形成责任感

对比:

- □ break school rules   违反学校的规定

- □ unacceptable behaviour   不可接受的行为

7 their peers
他们的同龄人

- □ peer pressure   来自于同龄人的压力

- □ are in their formative years
  还处在性格逐渐形成的阶段

- □ often act on impulse   时常会冲动地行事

- □ are influenced by peer pressure
  受到同辈压力的影响

peer pressure（同辈压力）是英美校园里的常用短语。积极的同辈压力（positive peer pressure）可以促使青少年更努力地学习，更积极地参加体育运动和社区活动。

但是消极的同辈压力（negative peer pressure）却导致很多青少年为了显得"酷"而吸毒（drug abuse）、参与校园欺凌（school bullying）甚至参加帮派（join gangs）、卷入犯罪（are involved in crime）

- feel lonely and isolated　感到孤独而且被孤立

- succumb to peer pressure　屈从于来自同辈的压力

8 behaviour problems / behavioural problems
行为问题(这两个表达在英美中小学里都经常有教师使用，behavioural problems 的语气更正式一点)

- unruly students / disruptive students
  不守纪律的学生

- are involved with gangs and crime
  参与帮派和犯罪活动

对比：

- take responsibility for their own actions
  对他们自己的行为负责任

- have respect for their neighbours and communities
  尊重他们的邻居和社区

9 drop out of school
辍学

- lack self-control　缺乏自我约束力

- do not think about the consequences of their actions
  （青少年）不考虑自己行为的后果

- commit a crime / commit crimes　犯罪

　家庭对教育的作用

- become law-abiding citizens
  成为守法的公民

- become useful members of society
  成为有用的社会成员

10 prepare them well for adult life
帮助他们为成年之后的人生做好准备

- increase their independence
  增强他们的独立性

- develop a positive outlook on life
  形成积极的人生态度

- become responsible member of society
  成为有责任感的社会成员

- become productive member of society
  成为能够为社会创造有用价值的社会成员

- become contributing member of society
  成为能够为社会做出贡献的社会成员

议论文话题 **4**

科学和技术的发展

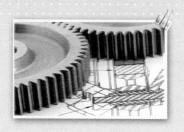

1 technological innovations

（名词短语）科技的创新

- □ technological breakthroughs　科技突破（名词短语）

- □ scientific discoveries　科学发现（名词短语）

2 advance scientific knowledge

推动科学知识的发展

（这个短语里的 advance 是及物动词）

- □ adopt new technologies　采用新的科技

  technology 一般是不可数的，但是当指<u>多种不同类型的</u>
  <u>科技</u>时，technology 允许使用复数形式

- □ meet new challenges　应对新的挑战

3 industrial automation

工业的自动化

- □ office automation　办公自动化

对比：

- □ perform repetitive tasks　从事重复性的劳动

4 **improve efficiency / boost efficiency**

提高效率

- □ time-saving technology　帮助人们节约时间的科技，例如：cars, dishwashers 等
- □ boost productivity　提高生产率
- □ reduce costs　减少成本
- □ meet consumers' needs　满足消费者们的需求

5 **are widely used**

被广泛地使用

- □ assembly lines　工业装配线
- □ mass-produced goods　被大批量生产的产品（名词短语）

6 **has transformed the way we communicate**

彻底改变了我们交流的方式

- □ has revolutionised the way we communicate
  彻底变革了我们交流的方式

7 **the information age**

（名词短语）信息时代

- □ the knowledge-based economy
  （名词短语）以知识为主导的经济，"知识经济"
- □ the technology-driven economy
  （名词短语）主要由科技推动的经济

8 **thin and lightweight**

很薄而且很轻的

- are portable and easy to use   很便携而且方便使用的

- are user-friendly   方便使用的,"用户友好的"

- modern conveniences   (名词短语) 泛指让生活变得更加方便的各种现代科技产品, 如手机、空调 (air conditioning)、微波炉 (microwave oven)、吸尘器 (vacuum cleaner) 等

9 farming technology

农业科技 (名词短语)

- factory farming   "工厂化养殖", 就是把农场饲养的动物 (livestock, 注意: 它在地道英文里不加 s) 关在很小的区域里, 喂给它们非天然的饲料, 让它们快速生长来压低成本。factory farming 是目前在英美很有争议的产业

- use chemical fertilisers   使用化肥

- increase crop yield   提高农作物的产量

- boost farming productivity   提高农业的生产率

- reduce hunger   减少饥饿现象

- increase food supplies   增加食品的供应

- prevent food shortages   避免食品短缺

- help to keep food prices stable
  有助于保持食品的价格稳定

对比:

- pose health risks to consumers
  对消费者的健康构成风险

- organic food   有机食品

- is safer and more nutritious   更安全而且更有营养

议论文话题 **5**

科技对生活的影响

1 **keep in touch with family and friends /**
stay connected with family and friends
和亲友们保持联系

- live away from home　与家人住在异地

- feel homesick　非常思念亲人

- video-chat（动词）/ video-chatting（动名词）
视频聊天

- make video calls　打视频电话

2 **use online resources**
利用网上的资源

- search engine　搜索引擎，例如：Google 和 Baidu

- find information quickly and easily
轻松、快捷地找到信息

- find information efficiently and effectively
高效地找到信息

- is fun and relaxing　有趣而且让人很放松

- is a useful educational tool　是一种有用的教学工具

□ is an important source of information
是很重要的信息来源

□ are just a few clicks away
（网络资源）只需要点击鼠标就可以轻松地找到

□ promote free exchange of ideas and information
促进思想与信息的自由交流

3 e-books / electronic books
电子书

□ are interactive　是有互动性的

□ provide many search options　提供很多的搜索选择

□ can change the font size　（读者）可以改变字号大小

□ take up much less space　所占用的空间远远更小

□ are easy to store and carry　方便储存和携带

□ meet their needs　满足他们的需求

□ read books on a screen　在屏幕上看电子书

□ may cause eye strain or headaches
有可能会导致眼睛疲劳或者头疼

4 paper books / printed books
纸质的书籍

□ the texture of the pages　纸张的质感

□ enjoy turning the pages　喜欢翻阅书籍的体验

科技对生活的影响

- □ are easier on the eyes （纸质书）不容易导致眼睛疲劳

  这个短语里的介词如果改用 for 也可以看懂，但 native speakers 就是习惯用 on

- □ can take notes comfortably
  （读者）可以舒服地做笔记

- □ prefer to hold a real book in their hands
  喜欢"手执一卷"的感觉

5 online shopping
网络购物

- □ online shops　网店

- □ physical shops ／ bricks-and-mortar shops
  实体店

  英文里还有 physical schools（实体学校，跟网校相对），physical classrooms（实体教室，和网络教室相对），physical books（实体书，跟 e-books 相对）等地道短语

- □ provide people with more choices
  （网络购物）为人们提供更多的选择

- □ is easy and efficient　轻松而且高效的

- □ is more eco-friendly　是更有益于环保的

- □ shop (*v.*) at lower prices
  （消费者）以更低的价格购物

- □ can easily compare prices　可以轻松地比较价格

6 distance education
远程教育

- distance learning courses　　远程教育课程
- can study at their own pace
  （学生）可以按照自己习惯的进度来学习
- improve efficiency and reduce costs
  提高效率并且降低成本

对比：

- traditional classrooms / physical classrooms /
  bricks-and-mortar classrooms
  传统的实体教室
- have lively face-to-face discussions
  进行生动的、面对面的讨论
- develop good learning habits
  形成良好的学习习惯
- form close friendships
  形成亲密的友谊（注意：这个短语里的 form 是动词）
- supplement their teaching with online resources
  （教师们）利用网络资源来作为对教学的补充

7 work from home / work remotely
远程上班

- have more freedom　　（员工们）拥有更多的自由
- have more flexible work schedules
  （员工们）有更灵活的工作时间

　科技对生活的影响

- can achieve a better work-life balance
  （员工们）可以在工作和生活之间获得更好的平衡

- save money on transport costs
  （员工们）节省交通方面的开支

- have more job opportunities
  （求职者们）可以有更多的工作机会

比较：

- reduce office costs   （雇主）减少办公室的开支

- can expand their labour pool
  （雇主）可以扩大招聘员工的选择范围

- video conference   视频会议

8 Internet addiction
"网瘾"

- lead to a sedentary lifestyle   导致缺少运动的生活方式

- lead an unhealthy lifestyle   过不健康的生活

- stare at a computer screen for many hours
  长时间地盯着电脑屏幕

- cause eye strain or headaches
  导致视力疲劳或者头疼

- damage their eyesight   伤害他们的视力

- increase the risk of obesity   增加患肥胖症的风险

9 interact with friends online
在网上与朋友交流互动

- social networking websites　社交网站（在当代英美，人们也经常用 social media 来指社交网站）

- video-sharing websites
  视频共享网站（例如：YouTube）

- photo-sharing websites
  图片共享网站（例如：Instagram）

- online community　网络社区

- make friends online　在网络上交友

- share information and exchange ideas
  分享信息并且交换想法

- participate in online forums　参与网络论坛里的讨论

- Internet celebrity　网络名人，"网红"
  （复数：Internet celebrities）

对比：

- in a virtual world　在一个虚拟的世界里

- cause social isolation　导致脱离社会的生活方式

- reduce face-to-face interaction　减少面对面的交流互动

10 rely too much on computers
过度地依赖于电脑

反义：

- reduce their dependence on computers
  减少他们对于计算机的依赖

- reduce their dependence on mobile phones
  减少他们对于手机的依赖

　科技对生活的影响

11 artificial intelligence / AI

人工智能

- □ can store more information
  能够储存更多的信息

- □ can process data more quickly
  可以更快地处理数据

- □ the human brain 人类的大脑

- □ are more efficient 更高效

- □ make fewer mistakes
  更少犯错误

- □ are controlled by computer
  programmes
  是由计算机程序控制的

- □ perform repetitive tasks
  从事带有重复性的劳动

- □ perform dangerous tasks
  执行危险的任务

- □ military robots 军事机器人

▲ 近年来在英美大受欢迎的会自己打扫房间的机器人 Roomba，有它帮忙 spring cleaning 可就轻松多了☺

—— Pat 摄

对比：

- □ cause unemployment 导致失业现象
- □ become self-aware 变得具备自我意识
- □ become completely autonomous 变得完全独立自主

12 video game consoles

电子游戏机(例如：Xbox One, PlayStation 4 和 Wii)

- interactive entertainment
具有互动性的娱乐

- increase hand-eye coordination
提高手眼协调的能力

- stimulate imagination and creativity
激发想象力和创造力

- online educational games
具有教育作用的网络游戏
（例如：online language games，online maths games，online quiz games 等）

- online intellectual games 网络上的益智游戏
（例如：online chess 网络象棋，online puzzles 网络拼图）

- team games / cooperative games 以合作为主的游戏

- discuss strategies and plans 讨论策略与计划

- improve their team-building skills
提高他们建设团队的能力

- try to progress through the levels
努力地通过游戏的各个级别

对比：

- competitive games
以竞争为主题的游戏

- try to get a higher score than their friends
力争比自己的朋友们的分数更高

103　　科技对生活的影响

□ become self-centered and insensitive to others
变得以自我为中心，而对别人却不闻不问

13 are highly addictive
（电子游戏）很容易让人上瘾

are addicted to video games 则是指玩游戏的人"对电子游戏上瘾"

□ cause lack of sleep　导致缺乏睡眠

□ lead to bad posture　导致不良的身体姿态

□ lead to a sedentary lifestyle
导致缺少运动的生活方式

□ cause eyestrain or headaches　导致眼睛疲劳或头疼

□ violent games　暴力的游戏

□ violent or sexual images 暴力或者色情的画面

□ glorify violence and killing　美化暴力与杀戮

□ make children more aggressive
让儿童变得更有攻击性

14 Internet fraud / online fraud　网络诈骗

□ online ID theft　盗用用户名

□ computer hackers　电脑黑客

□ email viruses　邮件病毒

□ malicious software / malware　恶意软件

□ security bugs　安全漏洞

议论文话题 *6*

科技对通讯方式的改变

1 means of communication
交流的方式

- □ text messages 手机短信

- □ video-chat（动词）/ video-chatting（动名词）
  视频聊天

- □ make video calls 打视频电话

- □ interact with family and friends 和亲友们交流互动

- □ faster and more efficient （电子邮件）更快而且更高效

- □ write letters 写信

- □ more sincere and thoughtful
  更真诚而且考虑得更周到的

- □ formal business letters 正式的商务信函

2 mobile phone users
手机用户

- □ keep in touch with family and friends /
  stay connected with family and friends
  与亲友们保持联系

- get help quickly in an emergency
  当遇到紧急情况时快速获得帮助

- browse the Internet on their mobile phones
  用手机上网

- pay bills from their mobile phones　用手机支付账单

- mobile games　手机游戏，"手游"

- fun and relaxing　有趣而且让人很放松

- is an important source of entertainment
  是一种重要的娱乐来源

  如果您发现自己在写手机话题时使用 mobile phones 的次数过多，那么也可以用 handsets 来替换它一两次

3 mobile phone radiation
手机的辐射（名词短语）

- rely too much on mobile phones
  （手机使用者）过度地依赖于手机

- excessive use of mobile phones
  对手机的过度使用（名词短语）

- pose health risks　构成健康风险

- may suffer from headaches and loss of concentration
  （手机的使用者）有可能会出现头疼、注意力不集中等症状

4 cause distractions for students
（或者 for drivers）
对学生（或者司机）构成干扰

- public places　公共场所

议论文话题 7
太空飞行

1 explore space
探索太空

- space exploration 对太空的探索（名词短语）
- space tourism 太空旅游业（名词短语）
- involve high risks 涉及到很高的风险
- involve huge costs 涉及到巨额的费用
- increase the burden on taxpayers 加重纳税人的负担
- have more important concerns
  （政府）还有更急需关注的问题
- space junk / space waste 太空垃圾
- pollute space 污染太空

2 satisfy human curiosity
满足人类的好奇心

- space missions 航天计划
- manned missions 载人航天计划
- Mars missions 火星探测计划
- scientific discoveries 科学发现
- space-related inventions 和太空探索有关的科技发明

  与太空探索直接相关的科技发明有 pacemakers（心脏起搏器）、scratch-resistant lenses（防划镜片）和 smoke detectors（烟雾探测器）等

太空飞行

- □ perform scientific experiments in space
  在太空进行科学实验

- □ expand human knowledge about space
  扩展人类关于太空的知识

- □ broaden human knowledge about other planets
  扩展人类关于其它行星的知识

- □ inspire children to explore science and technology
  激励孩子们去探索科学和技术

- □ inspiring achievements　令人鼓舞的成就

3 weather satellite
气象卫星

- □ provide reliable weather forecasts
  提供可靠的天气预报

  地道英文里还有 provide reliable information，provide reliable healthcare services，provide reliable public transport services 等短语

4 communications satellite
通讯卫星

这个短语里的 communication 习惯用复数

- □ satellite television　卫星电视

- □ provide a wide variety of channels
  提供多种多样的频道

5 the Global Positioning System（GPS）
全球卫星定位系统

- □ make driving easier and more comfortable
  让开车变得更轻松、更舒适

議論文話題 **8**

看电视和上网

1 **is fun and relaxing**

（看电视）有趣而且让人很放松

- □ watching television together

  一起看电视（动名词短语）

- □ is a good family bonding activity

  （一起看电视）是很好的增强家庭凝聚力的活动

  对比：

- □ is passive entertainment

  是被动的娱乐

- □ spend too much time watching television

  用过多的时间看电视

  spend too much time using a computer 使用电脑的时间
  过长，spend too much time playing video games 用过多
  的时间打游戏

- □ lead to a sedentary lifestyle

  导致缺少运动的生活方式

- □ watch less television / reduce television viewing

  减少看电视的时间

- watching television together
  一起看电视（动名词短语）

> **英语文化里的两种娱乐**
>
> - passive entertainment
>   被动型娱乐，例如看电视，因为通常并不需要很多的思考（do not require much thought），像 Sherlock 那样的 TV series 毕竟是少数
> - active entertainment
>   主动型的娱乐，例如读书、下棋等，因为它们需要人们很积极地思考（think actively），或者积极地参与（play active roles）

2 is a good way to reduce stress / is a good way to relieve stress
是很好的减压方式

`对比：`

- have a fast-paced lifestyle　生活的节奏很快
- have a stressful lifestyle　生活的压力很大

3 provide a wide range of channels
提供多种多样的频道

- cable television　有线电视
- satellite television　卫星电视

4 provide a wide variety of shows
提供多种多样的节目

□ are informative and educational
（一些电视节目）是信息量很大而且很有知识性的

□ are entertaining and enjoyable
是娱乐性很强而且令人愉快的

□ provide good topics of conversation
提供有趣的谈话话题

5 attract many viewers
吸引很多的观众

□ increase their popularity
提高（电视节目的）收视率

6 surf the Internet browse the Internet
上网（同样也很地道的表达）

□ have easy access to…
可以很方便地获取（某种资源）

7 violence on television
电视上的暴力内容（名词短语）

□ regulate violence in the media
（政府）严格地监管媒体里面的暴力内容

□ film rating system
电影的分级制度

看电视和上网

□ reduce their exposure to violence in the media
减少他们接触到媒体暴力的机会

对比：

□ copy the behavior that they see in the media
（青少年）模仿他们在媒体里看到的行为

□ cannot easily tell the difference between reality and fantasy
（青少年）不太会分辨现实生活和幻想之间的区别

8 **violent or sexual images**
暴力或色情的画面（名词短语）

□ offensive language
（名词短语）污言秽语，
"粗口"

□ make children aggressive
让儿童变得具有攻击性

广 告

1 **make products more attractive to consumers**
让产品对消费者们更有吸引力

- □ is an important marketing tool
  是很重要的市场营销工具

- □ inform consumers about new products or services
  告知消费者们关于新产品或者服务的资讯

- □ help consumers make informed choices
  帮助消费者们根据可靠的信息做出选择

- □ boost the sales of the advertised products
  提升所宣传的产品的销量

- □ encourage people to associate the advertised product
  with an attractive lifestyle　鼓励人们把所宣传的产品
  与有吸引力的生活方式联系到一起

  还可以更具体地写 encourage people to associate the
  advertised product with **a healthy lifestyle**（健康的生活方
  式）, encourage people to associate the advertised
  product with **a wealthy lifestyle**（富有的生活方式）等

2 commercial breaks
插播广告的时间段

电视或者收音机播放的广告经常被称为 television commercials 和 radio commercials

- □ interrupt TV programmes
  （广告）中断电视节目的播出

- □ spoil people's enjoyment of the show
  （广告）让看节目的人感到很扫兴

比较：

- □ pop-up advertising windows　网页上面弹出的广告

- □ promotional flyers　促销用的传单

- □ classified advertisements　报纸上的分类小广告

3 are creative and entertaining
很有创意而且娱乐性很强的

- □ is an important source of entertainment
  是一种很重要的娱乐来源

- □ is an indispensable part of our lives
  是我们生活里不可缺少的一个部分

4 advertising campaigns
大规模的广告系列宣传活动

campaign 的原意为战役，但在 IELTS 作文里，它总是用来指**大规模的系列宣传活动**。在政府话题里您还能看到更多的 campaigns

5 **advertising aimed at children**

专门针对儿童的广告

□ attract children's attention

(垃圾食品、玩具的广告)吸引儿童的注意

□ are easily influenced by advertising /
are easily swayed by advertising

(儿童们)很容易受到广告的影响

动词 sway 是指影响某人的选择,常用在 **are easily swayed by**...这个固定搭配里

□ regulate advertising aimed at children

(政府)严格地监管针对儿童的广告

Pat 注意到有很多中国同学喜欢把 advertisement 和 advertising 当成同义词使用。其实,在地道英文里它们并不完全相同:

advertisement 是**可数名词**,an advertisement 是指一条广告,advertisements 是指多条广告。而 advertising 是**不可数名词**,是泛指广告这种宣传形式。例如:advertising costs (广告宣传的费用),advertising revenue (媒体来自于广告的收入),the advertising industry (广告产业)等等

---

6 **false advertising / deceptive advertising**

虚假的广告宣传(名词短语)

□ provide misleading information 提供有误导性的信息

广 告

- damage their reputation　破坏他们的声誉
- reduce customer loyalty　减少消费者对于品牌的忠诚度

对比：

- provide reliable information　提供可靠的信息
- help consumers better understand the advertised product
  帮助消费者们更好地了解所宣传的产品
- can help to build customer loyalty
  有助于建立起消费者们对品牌的忠诚度

7 the advertising industry
广告产业，广告业

- employ many people　雇佣大量的员工
- is an important source of employment
  是重要的就业机会来源
- contribute to the economy　为经济做贡献
- pay taxes to the government　向政府纳税
- is an important source of government tax revenue
  是政府税收的重要来源

8 are driven by profit
是受到营利目的所驱动的

- advertising revenue　媒体来自于广告的收入

对比：

- public-interest advertising　公益广告

9 try to persuade people to buy a product

（广告 advertisements 或者出现在广告里的名人 celebrities who appear in advertisements）努力劝说人们去购买某一产品

□ try to persuade people to follow the latest trends
努力劝说人们去追随最新的潮流

□ influence consumers' decision-making process
影响消费者们做购物决定的过程

对比:

□ have different incomes
（消费者们）收入不同

□ have different budgets
（消费者们）有不同的开支预算

□ have different tastes and preferences
（消费者们）有着不同的品位和偏好

广 告

议论文话题 *10*

新 闻

BREAKING NEWS

1 current events
时事

- international events 国际时事

- sports news 体育新闻

- business and financial news 财经新闻

- cultural and entertainment news
  文化和娱乐新闻

- inform people about important events
  帮助人们了解重要的事件
  (inform 是 information 的动词)

- is an important source of information
  是一种重要的信息来源

- is an indispensable part of our lives
  是我们生活里不可缺少的一个部分

2 news reports / news stories
新闻报导

- live news coverage
  (名词短语) 来自现场的新闻报导

3 **electronic media**

电子媒体（例如：电视，广播，互联网等）

□ provide up-to-the-minute news and information
提供非常及时的新闻资讯

对比：

□ print media
印刷媒体（例如：报纸和杂志）

□ cover subjects with greater depth
对选题进行更有深度的报导

□ help people to gain a better understanding of ...
帮助人们获取对于……更深入的了解

4 **international news agencies**

国际新闻社

例如 Reuters（路透社）和 the Associated Press（美联社）

□ multinational media companies
跨国传媒公司，例如：BBC, CNN, Bloomberg（主要
提供财经信息）

5 **fair and balanced**

公正的、不偏颇的

□ objective and reliable
客观的、值得信赖的

新 闻

- biased and unfair
  有偏见的、不公正的

- influence people's opinions and attitudes
  影响人们的看法与心态

- false news reports 假新闻

6 media sensationalism
媒体对于事件进行夸大渲染的倾向

- sensationalise news stories
  对新闻报导进行夸大渲染

- attract more viewers, listeners or readers
  吸引更多的观众、听众或者读者

7 influence public opinion
影响公众的意见（中性）

- provide reliable information
  提供可靠的信息

- help people to make well-informed decisions
  帮助人们做出基于可靠信息的决定（褒义）

- mislead the public 误导公众（贬义）

議論文話題 *11*

政府的权力和责任

1 regulate + 宾语

对 …… 进行严格的监管

- □ introduce laws to …　通过立法来……

- □ tighten the law on …　针对某事物制定更严格的法律

2 take measures to …

采取措施去……

近义: take steps to …

3 is practical and fair

（某个政策）是可行的而且公正的

- □ is likely to receive public support
  很可能会获得公众的支持

对比:

- □ is impractical and unfair
  是缺乏可行性而且也是不公正的

- □ a short-sighted policy　一个短视的政策

4 armed forces
武装力量

- military spending　军费的开支
- military technology　军事科技
- protect national security　保护国家的安全

对比：

- threaten national security　威胁国家的安全
- tensions and conflicts　紧张关系和冲突
- weapons of mass destruction　大规模杀伤性武器

5 police forces
警力

- reduce crime　减少犯罪
- prevent crime　预防犯罪
- protect the public　保护公众
- maintain law and order　维护法律和秩序

对比：

- threaten people's safety　威胁人们的安全

  threaten 的意思也可以用短语 pose a threat to …来表示

- increase people's fear of crime
  增加人们对于犯罪的恐惧感
- cause social unrest　导致社会的动荡不安

6 a free and fair society
一个自由的、公正的社会

- an open and democratic government
  一个开明的、民主的政府

- should be a personal choice   应该是个人的选择

- should be free from government interference
  不应该受到政府的干预，应当免受政府的干预

对比：

- restrict people's freedom   限制人们的自由

- goes against the values of a free and fair society
  （某种政策）违背了一个自由、公正的社会的价值观

7 improve public health
增进公众的健康

- run campaigns to encourage people to …
  组织大规模的系列宣传活动以鼓励人们去做某事

  run 在这个短语里是指举办，campaigns 是指大规模的系列宣传活动

- promote healthy lifestyles
  促进健康的生活方式

- exercise regularly
  经常锻炼身体

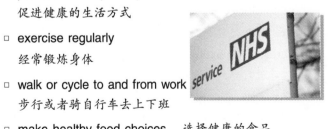

- walk or cycle to and from work
  步行或者骑自行车去上下班

- make healthy food choices   选择健康的食品

政府的权力和责任

8 protect their cultural heritage
保护他们的文化传承

- promote their cultural heritage
  推广他们的文化传承

- attract tourists　吸引游客

- create jobs　创造就业

不要挖空心思去寻找"抢眼球"的写法，create jobs 在英语国家里就是表示"创造就业"最地道的写法。如果非要再"难"一点，可以写 create employment opportunities

9 private companies
私人公司

- are driven by profit　是受营利目的所驱动的

- make large profits　获取高额的利润

- maximise profits　实现利润的最大化

- minimise costs　实现成本开支的最小化

对比：

- meet their social responsibilities
  （公司）履行它们的社会责任

- protect the public interest
  （政府）保护公众的利益

- promote open and fair competition
  （政府）促进公开、公平的竞争

議論文話題 *12*
政府的经费分配

1 invest money in ... / spend money on ... /
allocate money to ＋ 某类人或机构／
allocate money for ＋ 某类用途
为（某个领域）拨款

> **对比：**
>
> □ are under-funded
>   （学校、博物馆、美术馆等）资金不足
>
> □ are under-staffed
>   （学校、博物馆、美术馆等）人员配备不足

2 give financial support to ...
为……提供资助

□ face financial difficulties　遇到财务方面的困难

□ ensure equal opportunities for all students /
  ensure equality in education
  （政府、学校等）确保学生们受教育的机会平等

3 allocate resources fairly
公正地分配资源

□ give priority to ...　把某个领域作为当务之急

▫ **the government's spending priority**
政府优先拨款的领域（名词短语，如果有多个领域也可以把 priority 改成复数 priorities）

▫ **divert money from... to...** （政府）把资金从某一个领域改用到另一个领域，例如：divert money from space research to public services

▫ **have more important concerns**
还有其他更需要关注的领域

▫ **This money might be better spent on ...**
这项资金也许应该被更明智地改用于……

对比：

▫ **is a waste of public money**
（某类事物或某项投资）是对于公共资金的浪费

4 improve public services
完善公共服务

▫ **are vital to a country's development**
（公共服务）对于一个国家的发展至关重要

vital 的准确含义是 extremely important，除非您确信某事物真的是"至关重要"，否则就踏踏实实地写 important 好了。对雅思写作而言，语言准确比"惊艳"更重要

在英语国家里，public services（公共服务）主要是指：education（教育，特别是 public schools），healthcare services（医疗服务，尤其是 public

126

hospitals）, public transport services（公共交通服务）, environmental protection（环境保护）, state pensions（由政府发放的养老金）, unemployment benefits（由政府发放的失业救济金）, child benefits（儿童福利金，也就是传说中的"牛奶金"）和 national security（国家安全）

5 improve infrastructure
改进基础设施

- [ ] infrastructure improvements　对于基础设施的改进
- [ ] make the economy more productive
  让经济变得更高效
- [ ] make the economy more competitive
  让经济变得更有竞争力
- [ ] increase the competitiveness of the economy
  提高经济的竞争力

反义：

- [ ] reduce the competitiveness of the economy
  削弱经济的竞争力

6 are funded by the government
是由政府来资助的

- [ ] public healthcare system　公共的医疗体系
- [ ] public libraries and museums　公立的图书馆和博物馆

　政府的经费分配

□ rely on the government for money　依靠政府的资助

□ increase the burden on taxpayers　增加纳税人的负担

7 increase government revenue
增加政府的收入

□ impose a tax on sth.　对（某事物）征税

□ impose high taxes on sth.
对（某事物）征收惩罚性的重税

□ pay taxes to the government
（公司或个人）向政府纳税

□ is an important source of government tax revenue
是政府税收的重要来源

8 create jobs
创造就业

□ reduce poverty　减轻贫困

□ boost economic growth　促进经济的增长

□ raise educational standards　提高教育水平

□ improve the healthcare system　改善医疗体系

□ encourage innovation　鼓励创新

9 is provided by the state
（某种公共服务或者福利）是由政府提供的

在英国，当讨论由政府提供的福利时经常用 state 这个词来指政府，例如：state benefits（由政府提供的福利）和 state pensions（由政府发放的养老金）

10 low-income families

低收入的家庭

- ☐ live below the poverty line
  生活在贫困线以下

- ☐ unemployed people /
  jobless people
  失业的人们

- ☐ hunger and poverty 饥饿与贫困

- ☐ reduce social inequality 减少社会不公正

  高频短语 people in need 在地道英文里并不是泛指一切
  需要帮助的人，而是特指生活在贫困当中的人们

11 provide them with vocational training

为他们提供职业培训（注意 vocational 的前两个字母
是 vo）

对比：

- ☐ prepare them for employment
  帮助他们为就业做准备

- ☐ have a steady source of income
  有一份稳定的收入来源

- ☐ earn a living and support themselves
  依靠自己的劳动生活，自力更生

政府的经费分配

议论文话题 *13*

经济、消费与
幸福感

---

1 the growing gap between（the）rich and（the）poor

正在扩大的贫富差距

在这个短语里，把两个 the 写出来或者省略两个 the 都可以，都是地道、常见的英文

- low-income families　低收入的家庭

- live in poverty　生活在贫困当中

- live below the poverty line　生活在贫困线以下

- high-income families　高收入家庭

- reduce income inequality　减少收入不均

当表示不平等的现象时，地道英文里常会用到 inequality 这个名词。例如：income inequality（收入不均）和 gender inequality（性别的不平等）

2 are overpaid

收入过高

对比：

- should be better paid　应该得到更高的收入

- should be better appreciated　应该得到更多的认可

□ should be better appreciated and better paid
应该得到更多的认可和更高的收入

3 reduce poverty
减少贫困

□ create jobs　创造就业

□ reduce unemployment　减少失业

□ narrow the gap between (the) rich and (the) poor
缩小贫富差距

4 consumer society
崇尚消费的社会

□ consumer culture　崇尚消费的文化

按地道英文的习惯，这两个短语里面的 consumer 都不用所有格

□ international trade　国际贸易（名词短语）

□ technological innovations　科技的创新（名词短语）

□ the demand for new products
对于新产品的需求（名词短语）

□ have more shopping choices
（消费者们）有更多的购物选择

□ more affordable consumer goods
价位更合理的消费品

□ improve people's standard of living
提高人们的生活水平

□ **create more jobs**
创造更多的就业

□ **increase the government's tax revenue**
增加政府的税收

5 become too materialistic

变得过于物质化的，只在乎物质享受的

比如：韩寒的粉丝说郭敬明的粉丝 too materialistic（过于物质化的），郭敬明的粉丝则说韩寒的粉丝 too idealistic（过于理想化的）☺

□ **earn more money** 挣更多的钱

□ **money and possessions** 金钱和财产

□ **become easily dissatisfied with what they have**
很容易对自己已经拥有的东西感到不满足，不知足

□ **become selfish and greedy** 变得自私而且贪婪

6 develop unhealthy spending habits

形成不良的消费习惯

□ **buy things on impulse / buy things impulsively**
冲动地购物

□ **use credit cards irresponsibly** 不负责任地"刷卡"

use ... irresponsibly 是一个很有用的结构，我们还可以写出 use natural resources irresponsibly, use water irresponsibly 等地道短语

- find themselves deeply in debt
  发现自己深陷于债务当中

对比：

- save for the future
  为将来储蓄（注意：并不一定非要写 save money for the future）

- use credit cards responsibly
  负责任地使用信用卡

- develop healthy spending habits
  形成良好的消费习惯

- manage their budget well
  管理好他们的预算

- have a sense of financial responsibility
  在财务方面具有责任感

- improve their money-management skills
  提高他们的理财技能

7 use more natural resources
使用更多的自然资源

- use more energy
  消耗更多的能量

- cause damage to the environment
  对环境造成破坏

□ create more waste and pollution

产生更多的废料和污染

这个短语里的 waste 不是指浪费，而是垃圾、废料的
意思

8 status symbols

身份与地位的象征

□ luxury cars　豪车

□ designer clothing　名牌服装

这个看似简单的短语，其实才是表示"名牌儿服装"最
地道的英文短语

□ expensive mobile phones　昂贵的手机

□ equate wealth with happiness　把财富等同于快乐

9 the main source of happiness

幸福的主要来源

□ achieve happiness　实现幸福

□ fame and wealth　名望和财富

对比：

□ cooperation and sharing

合作与分享（名词短语）

□ maintain a good work-life balance

保持工作与生活之间的合理平衡

□ a strong commitment to family and work
对家庭和工作的强烈责任感

□ have a steady source of income
有一份稳定的收入来源

□ have a healthy lifestyle
遵循健康的生活方式

□ do volunteer work / do voluntary work
做义工

□ make donations to charities
为慈善组织捐款

□ actively participate in community activities
积极地参加社区活动

10 charity（复数：charities）/ charitable organisation
慈善机构

□ provide help to people in need
向贫困的人们提供帮助

□ make generous donations
进行慷慨的捐赠

交通和运输

1 public transport
公共交通

- improve public transport services
  增进公共交通服务的质量

- increase public transport facilities
  增加公共交通设施的数量

对比:

- the growing number of car owners /
  the rising levels of car ownership
  上升的车主人数

- private cars　私家车

2 rely too much on cars
过度地依赖汽车

对比:

- reduce their dependence on cars
  减少他们对于汽车的依赖

- drive less　少开车

▫ use public transport more often
更多地乘坐公共交通

▫ walk or cycle to and from work
步行或者骑自行车上下班

3 improve road safety
改善道路安全

【BBC 例句】There are many road signs that help to improve road safety in the UK

▫ upgrade the road system　对道路系统进行升级改造

▫ install red light cameras　安装交通灯监控摄像头

▫ install speed cameras　安装超速监控摄像头

▫ prevent dangerous driving　预防危险的驾驶行为

▫ drive safely　安全驾驶

▫ make traffic more efficient　让交通变得更高效

4 traffic volume / volume of traffic
交通量

▫ traffic pollution　交通污染

▫ car fumes / traffic fumes / exhaust fumes from vehicles
车辆的尾气

▫ traffic noise levels　交通的噪声等级

▫ road accidents / car accidents　交通事故

- improve public transport services　改进公共交通服务
- raise the vehicle tax　提高车辆税

5 traffic jam / traffic congestion
交通堵塞

【区分】traffic jam 是可数的，可以写 traffic jams 或者 a traffic jam，而 traffic congestion 是不可数的

- rush hour　交通高峰时间

- provide real-time traffic information
  提供实时路况信息
- reduce road accidents　减少交通事故
- reduce traffic jams / reduce traffic congestion
  减轻交通堵塞

6 break traffic rules
违反交通规则

- dangerous driving　危险的驾驶行为
- reckless drivers　不考虑后果的司机
- pay heavy fines　交纳很高的罚金
- do community service　从事社区服务
  (在英美很常见的一种对肇事司机 driving offenders 的惩罚方式)

138

- are sent to prison　被判刑
- deter dangerous driving　震慑危险驾驶的行为

地道英文里还有 deter crime （震慑犯罪）, deter criminals （震慑罪犯）, deter anti-social behaviour （震慑反社会行为）等短语

- install speed cameras
  安装超速监控摄像头
- install red light cameras
  安装交通灯监控摄像头
- prevent dangerous driving
  预防危险的驾驶行为
- raise public awareness of road safety
  提高公众的交通安全意识
- drive safely　安全开车
- drive more responsibly
  更负责任地驾驶

7 fuel-efficient cars
节能型汽车

- save fuel　节约燃料
- low-emission cars　低排量的汽车
- hybrid cars
  混合动力车（目前在英美最常见的是 Prius）

- electric cars　以电为动力的汽车（目前在欧洲和北美最常见的是 Nissan Leaf 和 Tesla Model S）

- reduce greenhouse gas emissions
  减少温室效应气体的排放

在地道英文里也常用 reduce carbon emissions 表示同样的意思。

8 airline company
航空公司

地道英文里也经常把这个短语直接写成 airline，复数是 airlines，可别当然地把它理解成"航线" ✗

- low-cost airlines／budget airlines
  提供低价航班的航空公司

- make air travel more affordable
  让乘飞机旅行的价格更容易承担

- air travel　乘飞机的旅行

- travel by air　乘飞机旅行（动状短语）

- travel more efficiently　更高效地旅行（动状短语）

- improve flight safety　增强飞行的安全性

- boost tourism　促进旅游业的发展

- increase greenhouse gas emissions
  增加温室效应气体的排放

- contribute to climate change
  进一步加剧气候变化

  contribute to 的后面跟积极含义的名词时是"做贡献"的意思，但后面跟负面含义的名词时则是"加剧"的意思

- plane crashes　空难事故

9 air transport

泛指航空运输(既包括客运也包括货运)

- more efficient　效率更高的

- more reliable　更可靠的

- passenger transport　客运

- freight transport　货运

- transport networks　运输网

- remote areas　偏远地区

- remote destinations　偏远的目的地

- areas inaccessible by rail or road
  铁路或者公路不能到达的地区

交通和运输

议论文话题 *15*
建筑、城市和社区

1 modern buildings
现代建筑

- □ building materials / construction materials
  建筑材料

- □ glass and steel 玻璃和钢材

- □ modern and attractive 很现代而且有吸引力的

- □ the function of a building 建筑功能

- □ efficient and effective 高效而且好用的

- □ comfortable and eco-friendly 舒适而且环保的

- □ are energy-efficient 是很节能的

- □ the structure of a building 建筑结构

- □ safe and reliable 安全可靠的

2 design buildings
设计建筑

- □ creative designs
  有创意的设计

- □ is visually pleasing
  是在视觉上很令人愉悦的

▲ Frank Gehry 设计的麻省理工学院 Stata Center ——Pat 摄

- □ the exterior of a building　建筑的外部
- □ attract people's attention　吸引人们的注意力
- □ the interior of a building　建筑的室内
- □ is nicely decorated　被装饰得很用心的
- □ the form-follows-function principle
  外在形式应该符合功能需要的设计原则

对比：

- □ compromise function for form
  为了追求好的形式而牺牲功能
- □ architects and building engineers
  建筑设计师和工程师
- □ real estate developers　房地产开发商

3 residential buildings
住宅建筑

residential 是 resident（居民）的形容词形式

- □ office buildings　办公建筑
- □ commercial buildings　商业建筑
- □ industrial buildings　工业建筑

4 tall buildings／high-rise buildings
高层建筑

【区分】只有非常高的"摩天楼"在地道英文里才能叫 skyscrapers，有些同学把小区里的高楼也称为 skyscrapers 是"小题大做"了

　建筑、城市和社区

- □ create a lively skyline　形成一道富有活力的天际线

- □ create an impressive skyline
  形成一道令人印象深刻的天际线

5 preserve old buildings / protect old buildings
保护老建筑

【区分】protect 既可以指保护某种资源，也可以指保护人的安全。

preserve 可以指保护某种资源，但是却不能指保护人的安全

- □ are protected by law　受到法律的保护

对比：

- □ demolish old buildings　拆毁旧的建筑

- □ make room for...　为……让出空间，这个短语里的 room 不是房间，而是指空间

- □ destroy historic fabric　破坏历史的脉络

- □ look similar　（现代的建筑）看起来很相似

- □ lack character　缺乏特色

6 buildings of artistic value
具有艺术价值的建筑

- □ are considered works of art　被视为艺术品

- □ historic buildings　具有历史意义的建筑

- □ famous landmarks　著名的标志性建筑

- □ cultural attractions　文化景点

- buildings of cultural significance
  具有重要文化作用的建筑

- give character to a city
  让一座城市具有鲜明的特色

  character 指电影、小说里的人物时是可数的，但指"鲜明的特色"时是不可数的

7 historic sites
重要的历史遗址

- are protected by law
  受到法律的保护

- tourist attractions
  旅游景点

- connect us to the past
  让我们关注、了解过去

8 form an important part of our cultural identity
形成我们文化特征的一个重要部分

form an important part of a city's history（形成城市历史的一个重要部分），form important part of our cultural heritage（形成我们文化传承的一个重要部分）

- enrich the local culture　丰富当地的文化

9 make a city more interesting and attractive
让一座城市变得更有趣、更有吸引力

- enrich the local culture　丰富当地的文化

- □ repairs and maintenance   维修和保养（名词短语）

- □ install modern equipment   安装现代的设备

- □ adapt old buildings to modern needs
  让老建筑适应现代生活的要求

10 urban areas
城市区域

- □ rural areas   农村区域

- □ urban living / city life   城市的生活

- □ rural living / rural life   农村的生活

- □ urban residents / city dwellers   城市里的居民

- □ rural residents   农村的居民

  urban 和 rural 都是形容词，绝不要错把它们当名词用 ✗

- □ enjoy the slower pace of life   享受比较慢的生活节奏

11 move to cities / relocate to cities
搬迁到城市里

由于任何原因搬迁都可以用 move，而 relocate 则一般是特指由于工作原因而搬迁

- □ earn higher salaries   挣更高的薪酬

- □ have more job opportunities   有更多的就业机会

- □ convenient public transport systems
  方便的公共交通体系

- □ better sports facilities   更好的体育设施

- more healthcare facilities　更多的医疗设施

- a wide range of entertainment and shopping choices
  多样的娱乐和购物选择

- provide a wide variety of cultural activities
  提供多种多样的文化活动

- museums and art galleries　博物馆和美术馆

- concert halls　音乐厅

对比：

- cause labour shortages in rural areas
  导致农村地区劳动力的短缺

- improve the infrastructure in rural areas
  （政府）改善农村地区的基础设施

- increase spending on rural schools and hospitals
  （政府）增加对农村学校和医院的资金投入

12 are overcrowded
过度拥挤的

- high housing prices　很高的房价
  （housing 是不可数名词，泛指住房）

- high crime rates　高犯罪率

13 are polluted
受到污染的

- car fumes　汽车尾气

- smog caused by car fumes　由汽车尾气导致的雾霾

□ cause health problems 导致健康问题

□ respiratory diseases 呼吸系统的疾病，例如：
asthma 哮喘，bronchitis 支气管炎，lung cancer 等

14 suffer from stress and anxiety
受到压力和焦虑的困扰

□ have a stressful life 生活压力很大

□ have a fast-paced life 生活节奏很快

□ face tough competition for jobs or promotions
面对激烈的就业或者升职的竞争

□ cannot achieve a good work-life balance
不能实现工作与生活之间的合理平衡

近义：

□ find it hard to achieve a good work-life balance

□ high living costs 很高的生活开支

□ rising crime rates 上升的犯罪率

□ frequent traffic jams 频繁的交通堵塞

□ lack a sense of community 缺乏社区感

□ do not even know their neighbours
（居民们）甚至不认识自己的邻居

□ feel lonely and isolated 感到孤独而且孤立

□ feel disconnected from nature
感觉自己的生活和大自然脱节

当 nature 表示"自然界"的时候，它的前面不能加定冠
词 the

15 city planners / urban planners

城市规划师

- □ divide cities into zones　把城市划分成一些区域

- □ residential areas　居住区域

- □ recreational areas
  休闲区域（例如有很多公园的区域）

- □ business districts　商务办公区

- □ commercial districts　商业区

- □ industrial zones　工业区

16 serve different purposes

（不同的区域）为不同的用途服务

- □ make the layout of a city easier to understand
  让一个城市的布局更清晰

  the layout of ... 是指城市、建筑、网站等的布局

- □ achieve efficient land use
  实现对于土地的高效利用

- □ make it more convenient for shoppers to compare
  goods, prices and services
  让购物者们可以方便地比较产品、价格和服务

- □ reduce pollution in residential areas
  减少居住区里的污染

对比：

- □ increase traffic volumes in some areas
  导致一些地区的交通量上升

- □ face tougher competition for customers
  （商店和餐馆等）面临更激烈的对于消费者的争夺

17 car-free zone / pedestrian zone
步行区

- □ pedestrian-friendly areas
  适合行人活动的区域

- □ become more pedestrian-friendly
  变得更适合行人们活动

  user-friendly（便于使用的），eco-friendly（有益于环保的）

- □ bicycle lane
  专供骑车的人们使用的自行车道

18 achieve sustainable development
实现可持续发展

- □ use resources more efficiently　更高效地使用资源

- □ reduce waste and pollution　减少垃圾和污染

- □ reduce people's dependence on cars
  减少人们对汽车的依赖

19 admission fees
博物馆的门票费

- □ charge admission fees　（博物馆）收取门票费

□ offer free admission　提供免费的参观

20 charge the same price regardless of nationality

（博物馆）不分国籍一律收取相同的票价

□ local visitors　来自当地的参观者

□ local residents　当地居民

□ pay taxes to the local government　向当地政府交税

□ foreign tourists / tourists from overseas　外国游客

□ spend money on local goods and services
（游客）消费当地的商品与服务

□ buy souvenirs　购买旅行纪念品

□ food and entertainment　食品和娱乐

□ contribute to the local economy
为当地的经济做出贡献

21 admission revenue

（博物馆）来自于门票的收入

□ government funding　来自于政府的资助

□ private donations　来自于私人的捐赠

□ revenue from gift shop sales
来自于馆内礼品店的销售收入

□ operating costs　运营的成本，运营的开支

22 enrich the local culture

（博物馆）丰富当地的文化

- □ attract many visitors （博物馆）吸引很多参观者
- □ boost tourism 促进旅游业的发展
- □ employ many people 雇佣大量的人员
- □ create jobs for local people 为当地人创造就业
- □ explore the local culture and history
  （游客们）探索当地的文化与历史

23 increase their collections

扩充它们的馆藏

- □ exhibition hall 展厅，英美比较大的博物馆里通常都会
  有多个 exhibition halls
- □ are on display （展品）被陈列，被展出

24 an important source of information

重要的信息来源（互联网、报纸、博物馆等）

- □ educational activities 很有知识性的活动
- □ hands-on activities
  允许参观者自己动手参与的活动
- □ interactive activities
  具有互动性的活动
- □ large touch screens
  大尺寸的触摸屏

- □ professional guides 专业的讲解人员

- □ recorded commentaries 关于展品的录音讲解

- □ educational exhibitions and lectures
  有知识性的展览和讲座

- □ are important educational resources
  是重要的教育资源

25 an interesting learning experience
一种有趣的学习经历

- □ are educational and entertaining
  既有知识性又有娱乐性的

❧ 英语国家最常见的博物馆类型 ❧

- □ science and technology museum 科技博物馆

- □ aviation and space museum 航空与航天博物馆

- □ folk art museum 民间艺术博物馆

- □ agriculture museum 农业博物馆

- □ history museum 历史博物馆

- □ military museum 军事博物馆（在一些英美城市还设有战争博物馆，例如伦敦著名的 Imperial War Museum）

- □ natural history museum
  自然史博物馆（主要介绍生物的发展和进化过程）

- □ fashion museum 时尚博物馆

- □ children's museum 专门为儿童服务的博物馆

□ wax museum　蜡像博物馆

26 provide a wide selection of books
（图书馆）提供内容广泛的书籍

□ book-based libraries / traditional libraries
以提供书籍为主的图书馆

□ suit their reading habits　适合他们的阅读习惯

对比：

□ computer-based libraries / digital libraries
以提供电脑资源为主的图书馆

□ save space　节省空间

□ can save many trees　能够让许多树木免受砍伐

□ need fewer employees　只需要更少的员工

□ reduce salary costs　减少在员工工资方面的成本开支

□ help people to find information easily
帮助人们很轻松地找到信息

□ is an important source of information
是一种重要的信息来源

27 community library
社区图书馆

□ improve children's reading skills
提高儿童们的阅读能力

□ provide cultural activities　提供文化活动

- free educational lectures
  免费的教育讲座

- enrich the cultural life of the community
  丰富社区的文化生活

  【Daily Mail 例句】These programmes encourage creativity and enrich the cultural life of the local community.

28 strengthen community connections
增强社区成员之间的联系

- build a strong sense of community
  建设很强的社区感

- develop good relationships with their neighbours
  与邻居们发展良好的关系

- actively participate in community activities
  积极地参加社区活动

- do volunteer work for their community /
  do voluntary work for their community
  为社区做义工

- raise money for their community
  为社区筹款

- improve community safety
  改善社区安全

- reduce crime and anti-social behaviour
  减少犯罪和反社会行为

建筑、城市和社区

议论文话题 *16*

工作和事业

1 job satisfaction
（员工）对于工作的满意度

- a high level of job satisfaction
  很高的工作满意度（名词短语，它的反义短语应该换掉哪个词显而易见）

- increase job satisfaction　提高工作满意度
  （它的反义短语是 reduce job satisfaction）

- a well-paid job　薪酬优厚的工作
  （名词短语，它的反义短语是 a low-paid job）

  在英国，a well-paid job 和 a low-paid job 更常用。而在美国，则是 a well-paying job 和 a low-paying job 更常用

- match their skills and interests
  （职业）符合他们的技能和兴趣

- gain new skills　（员工们）获取新的技能

- achieve their career goals　实现他们的事业发展目标

- feel a sense of pride and belonging
  有一种荣誉感和归属感

2 a friendly working environment
友好的工作环境

- provide a friendly working environment
  提供一个友好的工作环境

- are treated fairly　受到公平的对待
  (反义短语是 are treated unfairly)

- feel respected and valued
  感到自己受到了尊重和重视

- have equal opportunities for promotion
  (员工) 拥有平等的升职机会

- ensure equal opportunities for all job applicants
  (雇主) 确保每个求职者获得平等的机会

3 good working relationships
良好的工作关系

- effective teamwork / productive teamwork
  卓有成效的团队合作

4 encourage innovation
(雇主或者公司) 鼓励创新

- have more creative ideas
  (员工) 有更多有创意的想法

- achieve their potential
  (员工) 充分发挥出他们的潜力

对比:

- stifle innovation　压制创新

- perform repetitive tasks　从事重复性的劳动

工作和事业

- □ fall into a routine at work
  （员工）陷入照章办事的惯例里

- □ feel bored and unmotivated　感到无聊而且缺少动力

- □ feel bored and frustrated　感到无聊和沮丧

5 are well rewarded
（员工的努力）得到充分的回报

- □ good job performance　良好的工作业绩

- □ effetictive teamwork　有效的团队合作

- □ a rewarding job　一份很有回报的工作

- □ financial rewards　经济上的回报

- □ emotional rewards　心理上的回报

- □ keep them motivated　保持他们的动力

- □ improve employee morale
  提高员工们的工作积极性，提高员工们的"士气"

- □ make employees more productive
  让员工们变得更高效

对比：

- □ make employees frustrated　给员工们带来挫败感

- □ damage employee morale　打击员工们的工作积极性

6 clear career paths /
well-defined career paths
清晰的事业发展方向（名词短语）

- choose career paths that really interest them
  选择真正让自己感兴趣的事业发展方向

- provide good opportunities for career development
  （雇主或公司）提供良好的事业发展机会

- increase employees' loyalty to the company
  提高员工对于公司的忠诚度

7 job security
工作的稳定性（不能误解成"工作安全"）

搭配：“提升工作的稳定性"搭配动词 increase 或者 improve 都可以，"削弱工作的稳定性"搭配动词 reduce 或者 damage 都可以

- have high levels of job security
  （工作或者员工）有很高的工作稳定性

- a steady job   一份稳定的工作

- a steady source of income   一个稳定的收入来源

对比：
- have less job security   工作的稳定性较低

- have no job security   缺乏工作的稳定性

8 temporary employees
临时职工（它的反义短语是 permanent employees 固定职工，长期职工）

- have a wide range of experience
  拥有多种多样的经验

　　　工作和事业

- develop a wide variety of skills
  发展多种多样的技能

- choose jobs that interest them
  选择他们真正感兴趣的工作

- have more time for their personal interests
  有更多的时间用于自己的个人兴趣

  比较：

- are paid lower wages　被付给较低的薪酬

- earn less money　挣钱更少

- have less job security　工作的稳定性较低

- have fewer opportunities for promotion
  得到升职的机会更少

9 employee benefits
员工福利

- health insurance　医疗保险

- paid holiday（英式，有时也叫作 holiday pay）/
  paid vacation（美式）　带薪的休假

- sick leave（在英国有时也叫 sick pay）
  不扣工资的病假

10 manual jobs
体力工作

- manual workers　从事体力工作的工人

□ office jobs / desk jobs　脑力工作

11 stressful working conditions
压力很大的工作状况

□ cause stress and anxiety
导致紧张和焦虑

12 work long hours
长时间地工作

□ frequently work overtime
频繁地加班

对比：

□ achieve a better work-life balance
（员工）更好地实现工作和生活之间的平衡

□ have more flexible working hours / have more flexible
work schedules
拥有更灵活的工作时间

工作和事业

议论文话题 *17*

食品和健康

1 a healthy and balanced diet
健康的、均衡的饮食结构

在地道英文里，diet 前面最常搭配的动词是 have 或者 eat

- a low-fat and low-sugar diet　低脂肪、低糖的饮食结构

- eat more fruit and vegetables　吃更多的蔬菜和水果

- reduce the risk of heart disease　减少患心脏病的风险

- reduce the risk of high blood pressure
  减少患高血压的风险

- reduce the risk of obesity　减少患肥胖症的风险

2 an unhealthy and unbalanced diet
不健康而且不均衡的饮食结构

- have a fast-paced lifestyle　生活节奏很快

- a diet of fast food
  以快餐为主的饮食结构

- high-fat food　高脂肪的食物

- contain too much fat
  含有过多脂肪

- sugary drinks
  含糖量很高的饮料

▲ 为了考好 IELTS，喝一次 sugary drink 也不是罪……

- a high-calorie diet   高"卡路里"的饮食结构
- increase the risk of heart disease and high blood pressure   增加患心脏病和高血压的风险

对比：

- home-cooked meals   家里做的饭菜
- should display health warnings on their packaging （不健康的食品）应在外包装上面明示健康风险

3 become overweight
变得过重的

- childhood obesity   儿童肥胖症

4 a sedentary lifestyle
缺少运动的生活方式

对比：

- have an active lifestyle   保持经常运动锻炼的生活方式
- do more physical activity   从事更多的体力活动
- exercise regularly （英美通用）/ take regular exercise （英式）经常锻炼身体
- walk or cycle regularly   经常步行或者骑自行车
- brisk walking 健步走（近几年在英美很流行的健身方式）
- increase their physical activity 增加他们的身体活动量
- watch less television / reduce television viewing 减少看电视的时间

163

食品和健康

- keep a regular sleep schedule　坚持有规律的作息

- maintain good health　保持良好的健康状况

- improve their health and well-being　增进健康和幸福感（well-being 是名词：泛指健康、幸福的生活状态）

5 raise public health awareness
提高公众的健康意识

- health programmes on television　电视上的健康节目

- health and fitness magazines　健康杂志

- health websites　健康信息网站

- provide reliable health information　提供可靠的健康信息

6 raise health awareness among young people
提高年轻人的健康意识

- promote healthy lifestyles among young people
  在年轻人当中推广健康的生活方式

- develop healthy eating habits　形成健康的饮食习惯

- make healthy food choices　选择健康的食品

- have more home-cooked meals　多吃家里做的饭菜

- watch less television / reduce television viewing
  减少看电视的时间

- increase their physical activity　增加他们的身体活动量

- do outdoor sports / play outdoor sports
  进行户外运动

- boost the immune system　提高免疫机能

- can work more efficiently and energetically
  更高效、更有活力地工作
- reduce healthcare costs　减少医疗开支

7 frozen food
冷冻的食品

- canned food　罐装的食品
- packaged food　有外包装的食品

对比:
- fresh food　新鲜的食品
- is more nutritious　更富有营养的

8 is transported over long distances
(食品) 被长距离地运输

- food miles　(固定短语) 食品从被生产出来到被消费者购买的过程当中经历的运输距离。随着运输和食品保存技术的发展, food miles 正在不断上升
- have more food choices
  (消费者) 有更多的食品选择

对比:
- increase greenhouse gas emissions /
  increase carbon emissions
  导致温室效应气体的排放量上升
- contribute to global warming　加剧全球变暖
- contain chemical additives　含有化学添加剂
- food preservatives　食品的防腐剂

食品和健康

- cause health problems 导致健康问题
- pose health risks to consumers
  对消费者们构成健康风险

9 imported food
进口食品（名词短语）

- multinational food companies 跨国食品公司

对比：

- locally-produced food 当地生产的食品
- take away jobs from local farmers
  抢走当地农民的就业机会

10 genetically modified food / GM food
转基因食品

- genetic engineering technology 基因工程技术
- genetically modified crops / GM crops
  转基因的农作物
- increase crop yield 提高农作物的产量
- make food look more attractive 让食品看起来更吸引人
- are more resistant to diseases and insects
  （转基因农作物）对病虫害的抵抗能力更强

对比：

- disrupt the food chain 扰乱自然界里的食物链
- pose health risks to consumers
  给消费者们带来健康风险
- regulate genetically modified food / regulate GM food
  对转基因食品进行严格的监管

11 organic food / naturally grown food
有机食品

- □ is safer and healthier 是更安全而且更健康的

- □ is more nutritious 是更有营养的

- □ are produced without chemicals
  是未使用化学产品生产的

- □ distrust genetically modified food
  （消费者们）不信任转基因食品

12 have a fast-paced lifestyle
生活节奏很快

- □ work long hours 长时间地工作

- □ often work overtime 经常加班

- □ rely too much on fast food 过度地依赖于快餐

- □ too much television viewing / television addiction
  看电视过多的倾向

- □ Internet addiction 网瘾

- □ is damaging to their health / cause damage to their
  health 对他们的健康产生破坏

13 work-related stress
来自于工作的压力

- □ study-related stress 来自于学习的压力

- □ cause stress and anxiety 导致压力和焦虑

- □ cause frustration 导致挫败感

167

食品和健康

- □ reduce stress and anxiety　减轻压力和焦虑
- □ is a good way to relieve stress　是一种很好的减压方式

14 the healthcare system
医疗体系

- □ increase the burden on the healthcare system
  增加医疗体系的负担

对比：

- □ improve the efficiency of the healthcare system
  提高医疗体系的效率

15 healthcare services
医疗服务

- □ healthcare workers / healthcare professionals
  医疗工作者
- □ healthcare costs　医疗的费用
- □ medical technology　医疗科技
- □ medical advances　医疗领域里的进步（这个短语里的 advance 作名词，同类短语：technological advances）
- □ medical treatment　医学治疗
- □ previously incurable diseases　先前不能被治愈的疾病
- □ can be treated and cured　能够被治疗而且被治愈

  treat 和 cure 的含义不同：treat a disease 是指**治疗**疾病，是否能治愈不一定，而 cure a disease 是特指**治愈**疾病

议论文话题 *18*

体育运动

1 increase strength, speed and endurance
提高力量、速度和耐力

- improve flexibility and balance   增强灵活性和平衡能力
- improve hand-eye coordination   增强手眼的协调能力

2 physical abilities
体能

- strength-based sports
  主要基于力量的运动

- speed-based sports
  主要基于速度的运动

- endurance-based sports
  主要基于耐力的运动

对比：

- a positive attitude   积极的心态
- strong willpower   顽强的意志力
- strong team spirit   很强的团队精神
- perseverance and determination   毅力与决心

169

体育运动

□ fair play and good sportsmanship
公平竞争的意识和良好的运动员精神

3 team sports
团队运动

□ improve team-building skills   增进建设团队的能力

□ promote team spirit   促进团队精神

□ develop communication skills   发展沟通能力

对比：

□ individual sports   个人运动

□ build self-confidence   树立自信

□ increase their independence   增强他们的独立性

4 sports facilities
运动设施

□ stadiums and sports centers   体育场和运动中心

□ football pitch
足球场（英式英语，在美国则叫 soccer field）

□ tennis court   网球场

□ swimming pool   游泳池

□ exercise equipment in parks   公园里的健身设备

□ have a healthy lifestyle   遵循健康的生活方式

5 national sports teams

国家体育代表队

- boost national pride 提升公民的民族自豪感

- strengthen national pride 增强公众的民族自豪感

  strengthen（增强）是 strong 的动词形式，weaken（削弱）是 weak 的动词形式

- promote the country's image overseas
  向海外宣传该国的形象

- government funding 由政府提供的资金

- private funding 来自企业或个人的资金

- corporate sponsors 企业赞助商

- individual donors 个人捐款者

- talented athletes 有天赋的运动员

- achieve their potential 充分地发挥出他们的潜力

6 host the Olympic Games

主办奥运会

- the host country 主办国，东道国

- economic benefits 经济方面的益处

- attract tourists from around the world
  吸引来自世界各地的游客们

- create jobs 创造就业

171

- ticket sales　门票的销售

- advertising revenue　来自于广告费的收入

- Olympic medalists　奥运奖牌的获得者们

- inspire people　鼓舞人们，激励人们

- build understanding and trust　建立理解和相互信任

- promote peace and goodwill　促进和平与亲善

对比：

- the construction of Olympic venues　奥运场馆的建设

- security measures　安全措施

- increase the burden on taxpayers　加重纳税人的负担

- is a waste of public money　是对公共资金的浪费

- go over budget　超出预算

- cause financial loss　导致财政上的亏损

7 televised sports events
通过电视播出的体育赛事

- are televised live　被通过电视直播

- attract many viewers　吸引很多的电视观众

  television viewers 是指看电视的人们，而 sports spectators 则是指到现场观看体育赛事的人们

- slow-motion replays　用慢镜头进行的回放

- advertising revenue　来自广告费的收入

8 dangerous sports

危险运动

- involve high risks　涉及很高的风险

- risk their lives　冒着生命危险

- head and neck injury　头颈部的损伤

- hurt their knees　伤及膝盖

- are intense and extremely exciting
  是扣人心弦而又令人极度兴奋的

- provide a great sense of achievement
  带来非常强的成就感

- use their skills and experience to control the risks
  凭借他们自己的技能和经验去控制风险

体育运动

人口老龄化和老年生活

1 population ageing
人口老龄化的现象

- □ an ageing population   正在老龄化的人口

- □ the increasing life expectancy /
  the rising life expectancy
  上升的人口预期寿命

- □ increase the burden on the healthcare system
  增加医疗体系的负担

- □ increase the demand for healthcare services
  导致对于医疗服务的需求增多

- □ shortages of healthcare workers
  医疗工作者的短缺

2 retired people
退休的人们

- □ people of retirement age   退休年龄的人们

- □ working adults   工作的成年人

- □ a smaller working population   更少的工作人口

- ☐ low birth rates　人口的低出生率

- ☐ cause labour shortages　导致劳动力的短缺

- ☐ the state pension system　国家养老金体系

- ☐ may collapse　（养老金体系）有可能会崩溃

- ☐ increase the burden on taxpayers　增加纳税人的负担

- ☐ raise（或者 increase / extend）the retirement age
  （政府）提高法定的退休年龄

- ☐ encourage immigration
  （政府）鼓励其他国家的人向本国移民

3 save money for retirement
为退休存钱

- ☐ retirement savings　为退休养老存的钱，养老储蓄

- ☐ state pension　政府发给老人们的养老金

- ☐ employer-sponsored retirement plan　有雇主参与的员
  工养老金计划，例如美国著名的 401（k）plan

- ☐ rising living costs　上升的生活成本，上涨的生活开支

- ☐ healthcare costs　医疗的费用

- ☐ high inflation rates　很高的通货膨胀率

- ☐ threaten their financial security
  威胁到他们的财务安全（动词 threaten 的意思也可以
  用短语 pose a threat to ...来表示）

- ☐ face financial difficulties　遇到财务的困难

- ☐ have to retire later　只能更晚退休

□ work beyond the retirement age
(员工) 达到退休年龄之后还要继续工作

□ have a steady source of income
有一份稳定的收入来源

4 promote age diversity in the workplace
促进职工年龄的多样化

□ have more experience (年纪大的员工) 经验更丰富

□ are loyal and reliable 忠诚而且可靠的

□ are more patient and detail-oriented
更有耐心而且更关注细节

□ have stronger professional networks
有更强大的职业关系网

□ care more about job security
更关注职业的稳定性

□ hold conservative views on many issues
往往对于很多问题持有保守的看法

□ are reluctant to accept new ideas
不愿意接受新的想法

对比：

□ are more innovative (年轻的员工) 有更强的创新能力

□ are more open-minded 思想更开放的

□ are ambitious and energetic 有志向而且精力充沛的

□ have better computer skills 具备更好的计算机技能

- are more interested in career development
  更关注于事业的发展机会

- are more likely to take risks　更有可能会去冒险

- may lack practical experience　有可能缺乏实践经验

- may make rash decisions　有可能会做出鲁莽的决定

5 age discrimination / discrimination based on age
基于年龄的歧视

- have a bias against ...　对（某类人）抱有偏见

- generation gap　代沟

- lead to misunderstanding　导致误解

对比：

- bridge the generation gap
  在不同年龄段的人们之间建立起理解和沟通

  这个短语里的 bridge 是及物动词，同类短语还有 bridge cultural differences（在不同的文化之间建立起理解和沟通）

对比：

- build a sense of community　建立起一种社区感

- improve their corporate culture　改进他们的企业文化

- ensure equal opportunities for all job applicants
  确保所有求职者都能获得平等的机会

  还可以写 ensure equal opportunities for all employees，ensure equal opportunities for all students 等地道短语

6 live with their adult children
（老年人）和他们的成年子女住在一起

【BBC 例句】40% of parents in the UK have helped **their adult children** buy a home.

□ look after their elderly parents
（成年子女）照料他们年迈的父母

□ are loving and patient
（祖父母们）关爱孙辈而且很有耐心的

□ look after their grandchildren
（祖父母们）照看孙辈

□ help their grandchildren with homework
辅导孙辈们做功课

□ teach their grandchildren good family values
教给孙辈们良好的家庭价值观

□ teach their grandchildren about family history
给他们的孙辈讲述家族历史

□ share their wisdom and life experience with their grandchildren　与孙辈们分享自己的智慧和人生经验

□ bring them joy and happiness
给老人们带来快乐和幸福感

□ give them a sense of purpose and achievement
给老人们一种目的感和成就感

对比：

□ live apart from their adult children
不和他们的成年子女住在一起

- residential homes
  为老人提供食宿和卫生等服务的养老院

- nursing homes　也是养老院，与 residential home 的区别在于：nursing home 里通常都配有 24 小时的专职护士值班，所以住在 nursing home 里的很多是需要医护的老人

- trained carers　受过专业训练的护理人员

- qualified nurse　有专业资质的护士

对比：

- feel lonely and isolated　感到孤独而且孤立

- feel useless and unwanted
  感到自己毫无价值，不被别人需要

- feel bored and frustrated　感到无聊和沮丧

7 nuclear family

"核子"家庭，也就是只有父母与他们的孩子在一起生活的小家庭

- are more independent　更独立

- have more privacy and freedom
  有更多的隐私和自由

对比：

- extended family　三代甚至四代人住在一起的大家庭

- grandparents and parents　祖父母和父母

- high housing prices　高房价

- pay their mortgage 交住房贷款，"还房贷"

- help with housework 帮忙做家务

- share household tasks 分担家庭里面的各种职责

- working parents 工作的父母

- save on childcare costs 节省照看孩子的费用

- respect the independence and individuality of other family members 尊重其他家庭成员的独立性和个性

比较：

- have different ideas about child rearing
  （祖父母和父母）对育儿有不同的见解

- have different values and lifestyles
  有不同的价值观和生活方式

- tend to hold conservative views on many issues
  （老人们）往往对很多问题持有保守的看法

- lead to misunderstanding 导致误解

- cause family conflict 引起家庭纠纷

8 **give up their seats for elderly people**
（乘公共交通的年轻乘客）为老年人让座

- have walking difficulties 有行走方面的困难

- improve their mobility 让他们出行更方便

- electric wheelchair 电动轮椅

- ramps and lifts （建筑物的）坡道和电梯

9 high birth rates

高出生率（名词短语）

- control population growth / limit population growth
  控制人口增长

- birth control / family planning （名词短语）
  控制生育的措施

10 trace family history

追溯家族的历史

- build a family tree   建立一棵"家族树"
  这是英美家庭研究家族过去的历史最常见的方法：先
  在纸上画一棵大树，然后在每根树枝或者每片树叶上
  面写一个祖先的名字（或者贴一张照片），就可以形象
  地显示出他们／她们之间的关系

- is an exciting process of discovery
  是一个令人激动的发现过程

- satisfy their curiosity about their ancestors
  满足他们关于自己祖先的好奇心

- can better understand their family heritage
  可以更好地了解他们的家族传承

- family health history   家族健康史

- help people to prevent some diseases
  帮助人们预防一些疾病

人口老龄化和老年生活

議論文话题 *20*

女 性

1 gender stereotypes
认为不同性别就会擅长不同领域的思维定势
（例如认为男孩都擅长学习数学，女孩都擅长学习语言
的思维定势）

- □ the opposite sex　异性

- □ gender bias　关于性别的偏见

- □ ... is seen as the natural domain for boys（或者 for girls）（某个领域）被视为是男孩（或女孩）天生就更擅长的领域

- □ influence their course selection
  影响他们／她们对课程的选择

- □ make them frustrated　让他们／她们感到挫败感

- □ damage their self-confidence　打击他们的自信心

- □ lose motivation　失去动力

对比：

- □ choose subjects more freely　更自由地选课

- □ have equal opportunities to study what they want to
  （学生们）有平等的机会学习他们／她们想要学习的内容

□ achieve their potential
  充分地发挥出他们／她们的潜力

2 **traditional gender roles**
传统观念里认为的男性和女性各自应该承担的社会
角色

□ gender discrimination in the workplace
  职场当中的性别歧视

3 **gender equality**
性别平等

□ are treated fairly　受到公平的对待

□ are paid lower wages　被付给较低的薪酬

□ earn less money　挣的钱更少

　比较：

□ have equal opportunities for promotion
  （员工们）享有平等的升职机会

□ promote gender equality in the workplace
  （雇主）促进工作中的性别平等

□ improve gender balance in the workplace
  让工作单位里的男女人数更均衡

4 **male-dominated professions**
男性占主导地位的职业

□ firefighters (*n.*)　消防队员

女　性

- construction workers　建筑工人
- physically demanding jobs　对于体力要求很高的工作

对比：

- social and emotional skills
  社会交往和情感沟通的技能

- communication skills　沟通技能

- teamwork skills　进行团队合作的技能

- decision-making skills　决策能力

- patience and confidence　耐心和信心

- a positive attitude towards work　对工作的积极心态

- operate high-tech equipment　操作高科技的设备

- have equal opportunities and rights
  拥有平等的机会和权利

- choose careers that really interest them
  选择他们／她们真正感兴趣的事业

- achieve their potential　充分地发挥出他们／她们的潜力

5 are caring and patient
关心别人而且很有耐心

- nursing jobs　护理工作，其实在国外的医院里也经常
  会看到男护士，不过总数还是女护士远远更多

- primary school teachers　小学教师，英国的官方统计
  显示：在英格兰只有12%的小学老师是男性，而苏格
  兰的小学里只有8%的男老师

- tend to be more peace-loving

  （女性政治家）往往更热爱和平

6 low birth rates
低出生率

- will cause labour shortages　将会导致劳动力的短缺

- will increase the burden on taxpayers

  将会加重纳税人的负担

- may cause the state pension system to collapse

  可能会导致国家养老金体系崩溃

- will damage the economy　将会给经济带来破坏

- will hinder economic growth　将阻碍经济的发展

对比：

- should encourage people to have more children

  （政府）应该鼓励人们多生孩子

- increase child benefits　增加儿童福利，英语国家里的
  child benefits 是政府给小朋友们的福利金，也就是华
  人家长们常说的"牛奶金"

- encourage immigration

  （政府）鼓励其他国家的人向本国移民

7 delay parenthood
推迟要孩子，推迟当家长

- delay motherhood　推迟作母亲

- have busy careers　事业非常忙碌

- □ work long hours　长时间地工作

- □ earn money　挣钱

- □ cannot achieve a good work-life balance
　无法在工作和生活之间实现良好的平衡

- □ high housing prices　高房价

- □ rising child-rearing costs　上升的育儿费用

- □ take maternity leave　休产假

比较：

- □ have a higher risk of pregnancy-related problems
　（年龄较大的母亲）在怀孕期间会承受更高的风险

8 full-time mothers / stay-at-home mothers
全职在家带孩子的母亲

- □ stay at home to clean, cook and look after their children
　留在家里清洁、做饭和照看孩子

对比：

- □ working mothers　上班的母亲

- □ work full-time　全职上班

- □ work part-time　兼职上班

- □ work from home　在家远程上班

- □ high childcare costs
　高昂的请人照看孩子的费用（例如：把孩子送到托儿所
　nursery 或者请 babysitter 的费用）

- □ share parenting responsibilities
　（父母一起）共同分担培育孩子的责任

议论文话题 *21*

语 言

￼ **1** foreign language skills
外语技能

- □ the target language
  （外语教学中的）目标语言，学生需要掌握的语言

- □ become proficient in a foreign language
  熟练地掌握一门外语

- □ develop a good command of a foreign language
  很好地掌握一门语言

- □ bilingual skills　双语技能

᝕ **会外语的优势** ᝕

- □ can communicate in another language
  能够用另一种语言交流

- □ can make more friends　可以结识更多的朋友

- □ have more entertainment choices　有更多的娱乐选择

- □ are exposed to different cultures and lifestyles
  有机会接触到不同的文化和生活方式

- □ are more tolerant of cultural differences
  对待文化差异会更宽容

- □ are more open-minded towards other cultures
  对于其他文化有着更开放的心态

- □ can think more creatively　可以更有创造力地思考问题
- □ compete for jobs in a global market
  在全球化的就业市场当中竞争
- □ have more job opportunities　有更多的就业机会

2 study abroad
在国外学习

- □ prestigious universities　享有很高声誉的大学
- □ academic qualifications gained abroad
  在国外获得的学历

3 the dominant language
占主导地位的语言，主流语言

- □ a global language　一种全球通用的语言
- □ the expansion of English　英语的扩张
- □ international conferences　大型的国际会议
- □ international business meetings　国际商务会谈
- □ international trade　国际贸易
- □ the dominant language on the Internet
  互联网上的主要语言
- □ have access to more information
  （会主流语言的人们）可以获取更多的信息
- □ have more entertainment choices　有更多的娱乐选择
- □ have more educational and employment opportunities
  有更多的受教育和工作机会

对比：

- □ a minority language　仅有少量使用者的语言，非主流语言

- is only spoken by a small number of people
  只有很少的人说这种语言

- is losing speakers　正在逐渐地失去使用者

- an endangered language　一种濒危的语言

- may disappear in the near future
  可能会将在不远的将来彻底消失

- die out / become extinct　灭绝

- the language barrier　语言交流过程当中的障碍

- feel isolated　（说非主流语言的人们）感到很孤立

- are treated unfairly　遭受到不公正的对待

- is more than a means of communication
  （语言）并不仅仅是一种交流的方式

4 mother tongue / native language
母语

- give them a sense of belonging
  （他们的母语）给予他们一种归属感

- form an important part of their cultural identity
  （他们的母语）构成他们文化特征的一个重要部分

- help them protect their customs and traditions
  帮助他们保护自己的风俗和传统

对比：

- feel disconnected from their heritage
  （不再说自己母语的人们）感到与自己的文化传承脱节

- lose their cultural identity　失去他们的文化特征

语言

議論文話題 *22*

文化和历史

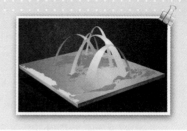

1 multicultural society
多元文化社会

- cultural diversity　文化的多样性
- people from a wide variety of backgrounds
  来自于各种各样不同背景的人们
- cultural differences　文化差异
- have different beliefs and values
  (多元文化社会里的人们)有不同的信仰和价值观
- are exposed to different cultures and lifestyles
  (多元文化社会里的人们)能接触到不同的文化和生活方式

- ethnic food　民族食品 (在英美，中餐、泰餐、印度餐等都是 ethnic food)
- ethnic clothing　民族服装
- different customs and traditions　不同的风俗和传统
- attract many tourists
  吸引很多的游客

▲ 多元文化社会的缩影：在这 5 个参加活动的年轻人里，有一个非裔，一个意大利裔，一个俄罗斯裔，一个荷兰与丹麦混血，一个英国、爱尔兰与法国混血，还有照片的华裔拍摄者——Pat

2 build understanding and trust
建设理解和信任

- □ live in harmony with each other　彼此之间和睦相处

- □ have equal educational and employment opportunities
  享有平等的受教育和就业机会

对比:

- □ cause barriers to communication
  (文化差异) 导致沟通过程中的障碍

  【搭配】"减少"沟通过程里的文化障碍可以用动词
  reduce, "克服"沟通过程当中的文化障碍可以用动词
  overcome

- □ lead to misunderstanding　导致误解

3 discrimination at school or in the workplace
在学校或者工作单位中存在的歧视

- □ are treated unfairly　受到不公正的对待
- □ cause tensions and conflicts　导致紧张关系和冲突

对比:

- □ employ a culturally-diverse workforce
  (企业) 雇佣文化背景多样化的劳动力
- □ have more creative ideas
  (员工们) 有更多有创意的想法

4 new immigrants
新移民

- □ feel lonely and isolated　感到孤独而且被孤立

　文化和历史

- cannot speak the local language well
  不会熟练地说当地语言

- are paid lower wages
  被付给较低的薪酬

对比：

- provide them with free integration courses
  为他们（新移民们）提供免费的社会融入课程

- help them develop a sense of belonging
  帮助他们形成一种归属感

- help them integrate into society 帮助他们融入社会

5 cultural heritage
文化传承

- historic sites 历史遗迹

- traditional costumes 传统服装

- customs and traditions 风俗习惯和传统

- traditional moral values 传统道德观念

- traditional music 传统音乐

- form an important part of our cultural identity
  形成我们文化特征的一个重要部分

对比：

- feel disconnected from their cultural heritage
  （人们）感到与自己的文化传承相脱节

- lose their cultural identity 失去他们的文化特征

- erode their sense of cultural identity
  （全球化、外国文化等）削弱他们的文化特征

192

6 traditional values
传统的价值观

- traditional virtues   传统的美德
  （注意：values 和 virtues 的拼写区别）

- hard work   勤奋的劳动

  它是名词短语，而 hard-working 则是一个形容词

- have respect for their elders   尊敬长辈

  elders 是名词，指一个人的"长辈"。而 elderly 则是形容词，指"年长的"

- sincerity and kindness   真诚与善良

- honesty and integrity   诚实与正直

- patience and self-control   耐心和自我约束力

- frugality and moderation   节俭和做事适度的原则

- good family relationships   良好的家庭关系

- a strong commitment to family and work
  对工作和家庭的强烈责任感

- a strong sense of what is right and wrong
  明确的是非观念

- develop a sense of responsibility towards their community   形成对于社区的责任感

  a sense of responsibility towards their school, a sense of responsibility towards their country, a sense of responsibility towards their own safety 都是地道又实用的短语

- live in harmony with nature   与自然界和谐相处

文化和历史

□ follow rules without questioning them
不带任何质疑地遵从规定

7 are more independent
（当代的青少年）更加独立

□ are more innovative　更具有创新性

□ are open-minded and creative　思想开放、有创造力

□ are exposed to many new ideas　能接触到很多新的想法

□ have the courage to challenge old ideas
具有挑战陈旧想法的勇气

□ will compete for jobs in a global market
将会在全球化的就业市场上竞争

□ are more likely to accept different views and
lifestyles　更有可能接受不同的观点和生活方式

8 traditional lifestyles / traditional ways of life
传统的生活方式

□ threaten traditional lifestyles　威胁到传统的生活方式

□ mass-produced products　大批量生产的产品

对比：

□ keep traditions alive　保持传统延续下去

□ hand-made goods　手工制作的商品

9 historical events
历史事件

□ historical figures　历史人物

- historical periods　历史时期

- connect us to the past　让我们关注、了解过去

- give us a collective memory　给我们一种共同的记忆

- form an important part of our cultural identity
  构成我们文化特征的一个重要部分

- is a rich source of inspiration for
  artists　是艺术家们创作灵感的
  重要源泉

- wars and conflicts in history
  历史上的战争和冲突

- help today's leaders avoid the
  same mistakes
  帮助当代的领导者们避免再犯同样的错误

- help them make better plans and decisions
  帮助他们更好地制定计划与决策

- promote international peace and understanding
  促进国际和平与理解

- help people to understand and solve social problems
  帮助人们理解并解决社会问题

对比：

- feel disconnected from their heritage
  (不了解历史的人们) 感到和自己的文化传承相脱节

10 study history
学习历史

- world history　世界历史
- national history　国家历史

- local history　当地历史
- political history　政治史
- social history　社会史
- art history　艺术史
- is informative and interesting
  （历史课）是信息量很大而且又很有趣的
- improve students' analytical skills
  提高学生们的分析能力
- sharpen their critical-thinking skills
  增强他们的辨证思维能力
- develop moral judgement　发展道德判断力
- help them better understand social change
  帮助他们更好地理解社会变革
- gain a better understanding of their culture
  更深入地了解本国文化
- famous historical quotes　历史人物的名言
- draw inspiration from history　从历史当中汲取灵感

对比：

- historians
  历史学家们

- have different values
  有着不同的价值观
- tend to have different views on the same event
  往往对同一事件持有不同的看法
- may contain bias　（历史书里的信息）可能含有偏见
- may be misleading　可能是有误导性的

议论文话题 *23*

艺 术

1 **works of art** 艺术品

（尤其常指绘画、雕塑等视觉艺术品，它的单数形式是 a work of art）

- □ visual arts　视觉艺术

  【实例】painting 绘画, sculpture 雕塑, photography 摄影和 graphic design 平面设计

- □ art museums / art galleries
  艺术馆，尤其常指美术馆

- □ art exhibitions　艺术展

- □ literary works　文学作品

- □ performing arts
  表演艺术，例如：ballet 芭蕾舞和 opera 歌剧

- □ folk art　民间艺术（native speakers 使用这个短语时通常习惯用单数）

2 **develop their artistic skills**
发展他们的艺术才能

- □ encourage imagination and creativity
  （艺术课）激发想象力和创造力

艺 术

- achieve their artistic potential
  （学生）充分发挥出他们的艺术潜能

- have more innovative ideas
  （喜欢艺术的人）有更多具有创新性的想法

- express their feelings creatively
  用富有创意的方式来表达他们的情感

- reduce stress and anxiety
  （音乐、艺术活动）减少压力和焦虑

- fun and relaxing
  有趣而且让人很放松

3 the art industry
艺术产业

- create jobs   创造就业

- attract many tourists   吸引很多的游客

- contribute to the economy   为经济做出贡献

- is an important source of government tax revenue
  是政府税收的重要来源

4 give financial support to artists
为艺术家们提供资助

- painters, sculptors and musicans
  画家，雕塑家与音乐家

- receive financial support from the state
  （艺术家们）从政府获得资助

- government funding   来自政府的资助

- have more important concerns
  （政府）还有更急需关注的领域

- respect artists' freedom of expression
  （政府）尊重艺术家的表达自由

- private donations　来自于公司或个人的捐赠

- sell their artistic creations
  （艺术家）出售他们的艺术创作

- earn money　挣钱

- art lovers and art collectors　艺术爱好者和收藏家们

5 public art /
works of art displayed in public spaces
公共艺术，在公共场所中陈列的艺术品

英美最常见的公共艺术形式包括：sculptures（可以指任何形式的雕塑），statues（通常是指人或动物的雕像），monuments（纪念碑），murals（壁画）以及 well-designed street furniture

- streets, squares and parks　街道、广场和公园

- give character to a city　让一座城市具有鲜明的特色

  character 指电影、小说里的人物时是可数的，但指"鲜明的特色"时是不可数的

- statues of famous people in the city's history
  城市历史上的著名人物塑像

- educate people about the city
  帮助人们了解自己所在的城市

□ promote a sense of pride in the city
促进人们对所在城市的自豪感

□ attract many tourists　吸引大量的游客

□ enrich the cultural life of cities　丰富城市的文化生活

□ bring art into people's everyday life
把艺术带进人们的日常生活里

□ can relieve stress
（听音乐，看艺术表演等）可以减轻压力

□ anti-war works of art　反战的艺术品

□ promote peace and goodwill　促进和平与亲善

□ works of art made from recycled materials
用回收材料制作成的艺术品

□ promote environmental awareness　促进环保意识

6 traditional music
传统音乐

□ folk music　民间音乐

□ international music　国际流行音乐

□ reduce stress and anxiety　减轻压力和焦虑

□ express emotions　表达情感

□ inspire people　鼓舞人们

□ lift people's spirits　振奋人们的精神

□ is an important form of expression
是一种重要的表达方式

□ is a universal language　是人类共通的语言

- build connections among people
  在人与人之间建立起联系

- transcend cultural boundaries
  (好的音乐) 超越文化的界限

- is an indispensable part of our lives
  是我们生活里不可缺少的一个部分

7 musical instruments
乐器

- play musical instruments　演奏乐器

- improve concentration and memory
  增强注意力和记忆力

- help them develop good learning habits
  帮助他们形成良好的学习习惯

8 the music industry
音乐产业

- create jobs　创造就业机会

- employ many people　雇佣大量的员工

- is an important source of employment
  是就业机会的重要来源

- pay taxes to the government　向政府纳税

- contribute to economic growth　为经济发展做出贡献

- music festivals　音乐节

- attract many tourists　吸引很多的游客

艺　术

全球化

1 build understanding and trust
建立理解与相互信任

- □ work closely together 紧密地合作

- □ international cooperation 国际合作（名词短语）

- □ tackle global problems 努力解决影响全球的问题（在 problems 前面还可以写 economic，environmental 等让论证变得更具体）

- □ promote international peace and understanding 促进国际和平与理解

2 imported goods
进口的商品（名词短语）

- □ domestically-produced goods 本国生产的商品

- □ locally-produced goods 当地生产的商品

- □ international trade 国际贸易

- □ is / are mutually beneficial 是互利的，是能让双方都受益的

- □ promote healthy competition 促进良性的竞争

- □ attract foreign investment 吸引外资

3 **encourage immigration**

（政府）鼓励其他国家的人向本国移民

□ ease labour shortages　减轻劳动力的短缺

4 **multinational corporations**

跨国公司

□ are globally operated　是在世界范围内运营

□ their global expansion　它们在全球的扩张

□ are mass-produced　（商品）被大批量地生产

□ are shipped around the world
（商品）被运往世界各地

□ have the advantage of scale
拥有大企业的优势，拥有规模经济的优势

□ dominate the local market　控制当地的市场

□ drive their local competitors out of business
导致它们在当地的竞争者难以生存

对比：

□ employ local people　雇佣当地的员工

□ are paid fairly　（当地员工）获得公平的报酬

5 **lead similar lifestyles**

（不同地方的人们）过着相似的生活

□ share the same fashions and brands
分享相同的时尚和品牌

全球化

- ☐ threaten cultural diversity　威胁文化的多样性
- ☐ erode their sense of cultural identity
  削弱他们的文化认同感

对比:

- ☐ show respect to the local culture
  体现出对当地文化的尊重

- ☐ show sensitivity to the local culture
  体现出对于当地文化的敏锐体察

6 multinational media companies
跨国传媒公司

【实例】BBC, CNN, Walt Disney
以及 Time Warner

- ☐ satellite television　卫星电视
- ☐ watch the same films and
  television programmes
  看相同的电影和电视节目

7 international aid
国际援助（名词短语）

- ☐ donor countries　援助国
- ☐ industrialised countries　工业化国家

在全球化类考题里，您可以把 industrialised countries 和
developed countries（发达国家）这两个名词短语作为
近义短语来替换使用

- recipient countries　受援国

- developing countries　发展中国家

- the international community　国际社会

  中文里所说的"国际社会"不能写成 the international society ✗

8 emergency aid
紧急援助（名词短语）

- natural disasters or conflict　自然灾害或冲突

- humanitarian aid　人道主义援助

- food aid　食品援助

- medical aid　医疗援助

- medical teams　医疗队

9 financial aid
财政援助（即资金援助）

- buy food and medicine　购买食品和药品

- reduce hunger and disease　减少饥饿和疾病

- reduce starvation and extreme poverty
  减少极度饥饿与贫困

对比：

- misuse the aid money　滥用援助资金（动宾短语）

- lead to more corruption　引发更多的腐败现象

全球化

10 development aid

发展援助(即以促进受援国的科技、教育、环境保护等
方面发展为目的的援助)

- create jobs　创造就业

- reduce poverty　减轻贫困

- technology transfer　从发达国家向发展中国家进行的
  技术转让（名词短语）

- technical training programmes　技术培训项目

- educational exchange programmes　教育交换计划

- improve infrastructure　改善基础设施

- improve education and health care　改善教育和医疗

- rebuild the economy　重建经济

- promote peace and goodwill　促进和平与亲善

- build an equal partnership
  建设一种平等的合作伙伴关系

- build understanding and trust
  建设理解与信任

- improve international relations
  改善国际关系

- reduce their dependence on
  international aid
  减少（受援国）对于国际援助的依赖

对比：

- is tied to political objectives
  被与政治目的挂钩，带有政治目的

206

旅游业

1 the tourism industry
旅游产业

- □ employ many people　雇佣大量的员工
- □ create jobs for local people　为当地的人们创造就业
- □ contribute to the local economy
  为当地的经济做出贡献
- □ is an important source of government tax revenue
  是政府税收的重要来源
- □ hotels and restaurants　酒店和餐馆
- □ museums and art galleries　博物馆和美术馆
- □ the local hospitality industry
  泛指当地的酒店餐饮等行业

对比：

- □ put pressure on local resources　对当地资源构成压力
- □ put pressure on the local infrastructure
  对当地的基础设施构成压力
- □ increase greenhouse gas emissions /
  increase carbon emissions
  导致温室效应气体的排放量上升

207

2 contribute to the local economy

为当地的经济做贡献

- buy souvenirs　购买旅游纪念品
- spend money on food and entertainment
  在食品和娱乐等方面消费
- accommodation and transport
  住宿和交通（名词短语）

3 festivals and ceremonies

节日和仪式

- attract more tourists　吸引更多的游客
- are over-commercialised　被过度商业化
- change their customs and traditions
  （当地居民们）改变他们的风俗和传统
- meet tourists' expectations　迎合游客们的期望
- threaten the local customs and traditions
  威胁到当地的风俗和传统

4 tourist attractions

旅游景点

- historical attractions　历史景点
- cultural attractions　文化景点
- natural attractions　自然景点
- make new friends　结交新的朋友
- expand their horizons　开阔他们的眼界

- experience different cultures and customs
  体验不同的文化和风俗

- gain first-hand experience of other cultures
  直接地体验其他文化

- get away from the stress of daily life
  从日常生活的压力当中解脱出来

- is a multi-sensory experience
  (旅行) 是多种感官的体验 (例如：参观景点、品尝当地的食品、欣赏当地的娱乐节目等等)

5 international tourists
国际游客

- foreign tourists / tourists from overseas   外国游客

- their destinations   他们的目的地

- local residents / local people   当地的居民

- interact with local people
  和当地的居民交流互动

- local communities
  当地的社区

- explore the local culture and history
  探索当地的文化与历史

- the host country   游客去旅行的国家

6 travel with a tour group
跟团旅行

旅游业

- stay in international hotels
  住在国际连锁的酒店里面

- only gain a superficial understanding of the local culture
  只获得对当地文化的粗浅的了解

对比：

- travel on their own　　自助旅行

- create their own itinerary　　（游客）自己设计旅行路线

- guide books
  旅行指南书籍（注意：中间的空格不要漏掉）

- travel shows　　旅游类电视节目

- travel websites　　提供旅游信息的网站

- learn about their destinations online
  通过互联网了解关于旅行目的地的知识

- hotels with local character　　具有当地特色的酒店

- explore the local culture　　探索当地文化

- better appreciate the local culture
  更充分地欣赏当地的文化

- interact with the local people　　与当地人交流互动

- learn more about their culture　　更多地了解他们的文化

7 explore the local culture
探索当地的文化

- interact with local people　　与当地人交流互动

- appreciate the local way of life　　欣赏当地的生活方式

- visit local attractions   参观当地的景点

- enjoy the local cuisine and entertainment
  享受当地的特色佳肴和娱乐

- show respect to the local culture
  体现出对当地文化的尊重

- respect local customs and etiquette
  尊重当地的风俗和礼仪

- behave respectfully in sacred places
  在当地人认为很神圣的地方保持举止得当

- are friendly and welcoming
  （当地人）是很友好而且欢迎游客的

  welcoming 意思是"欢迎来客的、热情好客的"，与
  You're welcome. 里面的 welcome 不同

- build understanding and trust   建设理解和信任

对比：

- are disrespectful to the local culture
  对当地的文化缺乏尊重

- cause tensions and conflicts
  导致紧张关系和冲突

8 travel for pleasure
为了休闲而旅行

- sightseeing tour   观光游（名词短语，它对应的动词
  短语是 go sightseeing）

- travel for business   为商务目的而旅行

211

旅游业

- family trips

  全家人一起的旅行（名词短语）

- are good family-bonding activities

  是很好的增进亲情的活动

9 responsible tourists
有责任感的游客

- respect local culture　尊重当地文化

- respect local customs and etiquette

  尊重当地的风俗和礼仪

- do not buy local products made from endangered animals

  不购买用濒危动物制成的当地产品

对比：

- create waste and pollution

  产生垃圾和污染

- damage the local ecosystem

  破坏当地的生态系统

- destroy wildlife habitats

  彻底地破坏野生动植物的栖息地

环　境

1 natural resources

自然资源

- preserve natural resources　保护自然资源

- use water responsibly
  避免浪费水（responsibly 是指"有责任心地"）

- conserve water　节约用水

- use natural resources responsibly
  有责任感地使用自然资源，避免浪费自然资源

对比：

- rapid population growth　人口的快速增长（名词短语）

- consumer culture　崇尚消费的文化（名词短语）

- industrial production　工业生产（名词短语）

- raw materials　原材料（名词短语）

- fossil fuels　化石燃料（包括 coal 煤，natural gas 天
  然气，oil 石油等）

- put great pressure on natural resources
  对自然资源构成很大的压力

- waste natural resources　浪费自然资源

□ use natural resources irresponsibly
不负责任地使用自然资源

□ an alarming trend   一个令人警觉的趋势

2 damage the environment
破坏环境

□ cause damage to the environment   破坏环境

□ introduce strict laws to protect the environment
（政府）通过严格的立法来保护环境

3 petrol-powered cars
以汽油为动力的汽车

□ use more fuel   使用更多的燃料

□ create more pollution   产生更多的污染

□ increase greenhouse gas emissions /
increase carbon emissions
导致温室效应气体的排放量上升

对比：

□ electric cars
电动汽车（例如：Tesla Model S）

□ are more energy-efficient   更节能的

□ **offer subsidies to electric car buyers**   （政府）为购买
电动车的车主提供补贴，例如：英国政府为每位购买
electric car 的车主提供£ 5, 000 的 electric car grant

4 **car fumes / traffic fumes /**
exhaust fumes from vehicles
车辆排出的尾气（名词短语）

- greenhouse gas emissions from factories
  工厂的温室效应气体排放（名词短语）

- contribute to global warming 加剧全球变暖

- contribute to climate change 加剧气候的变化

- cause the polar ice caps to melt
  导致极地冰盖融化（北极熊：polar bears）

- cause sea levels to rise 导致海平面上升

- damage the ozone layer 破坏大气臭氧层

- allow more ultraviolet rays to reach Earth
  让更多的紫外线到达地球

- increase the risk of skin cancer 增加患皮肤癌的风险

对比：

- reduce our carbon footprint 减少我们的"碳足迹"

  减少"碳足迹"是近年来在英美极为常见的环保概念，也就
  是减少由于开车、使用电器等所导致的温室效应气体

- control industrial pollution 治理工业污染

5 **pollute the air**
污染空气

- lead to acid rain 导致酸雨

- cause smog 导致雾霾

- make people sick 导致人们患病

- increase the risk of asthma, bronchitis and lung cancer　导致患哮喘、支气管炎与肺癌的风险上升

- cause damage to buildings　破坏建筑物

对比:

- reduce people's dependence on cars
  减少人们对于汽车的依赖

- drive less　少开车

- use public transport more often　更多地乘坐公共交通

- walk or cycle to and from work　步行或者骑自行车上下班

6 pollute rivers and lakes

污染河流和湖泊

- discharge waste into rivers　将废料排入河流里

  【BBC 例句】The factory was fined（被罚款）for discharging waste into the river.

- threaten aquatic life and public health
  威胁水生生物和公众健康

对比:

- introduce strict laws to control pollution
  （政府）通过严格的立法来治理污染

7 oil spill

石油泄漏事件，漏油事件（名词短语）

- threaten marine life　威胁海洋生物

- pose a threat to marine life　威胁海洋生物

8 log forests

砍伐森林

- □ cut down large numbers of trees 砍伐大量的树木

- □ destroy wildlife habitats 彻底地破坏动植物的栖息地

- □ disrupt the ecosystem 扰乱生态系统

- □ cause natural disasters 导致自然灾害

- □ dust storm 沙尘暴

- □ floods and droughts 洪水和干旱

- □ extreme weather conditions 极端的天气状况

9 clean energy

清洁能源(最常考的是 solar energy 太阳能和 wind energy 风能)

- □ renewable energy sources 可再生的能源

- □ promote the use of renewable energy
  促进对可再生能源的使用

- □ research on renewable energy 关于可再生能源的研究

- □ solar panel 太阳能电板

- □ wind farm 它不是"养风农场",而是指风力发电厂

- □ reduce our dependence on fossil fuels
  减少我们对于化石燃料的依赖

- □ alternative energy sources 替代性能源

- □ do not pollute the environment 不会污染环境

- □ achieve sustainable development 实现可持续的发展

环 境

対比:

□ rely heavily on weather conditions
  (太阳能和风能) 严重依赖于天气状况

10 build nuclear power stations
建造核电站

□ nuclear energy   核能

□ generate electricity without using fossil fuels
  发电但并不使用化石燃料

□ does not depend on weather conditions
  不依赖于天气状况

□ can help to reduce greenhouse gas emissions
  有助于减少温室效应气体的排放

対比:

□ radioactive nuclear waste   有放射性的核废料

□ cause health and safety concerns
  导致健康和安全方面的担忧

□ nuclear accident   核事故, 非常严重的核事故可以称
  为 nuclear disaster

□ nuclear weapons   核武器

□ may be obtained by terrorists
  有可能会落入恐怖分子手中

11 water shortages
水短缺 (名词短语)

□ the rising demand for water
  对于水的上升的需求 (名词短语)

- irrigation needs　灌溉土地的需要（名词短语）

- industrial production　工业生产（名词短语）

- household use of water 家庭对水的使用（名词短语）

- waste water　浪费水

- use water irresponsibly　不负责任地用水

- is becoming scarce in many regions
  （水）在很多地区变得稀缺

- water crisis　水的危机

对比：

- conserve water　节约用水

- use water more responsibly　更负责任地用水

- hand-wash and air-dry laundry　手洗并且晾干衣物

- improve water supply systems　改善供水系统的功能

- reduce water pollution　减少水污染

- control water pollution　治理水污染

- desalination technology　海水淡化技术（名词短语）

- convert seawater to fresh water　把海水转化成淡水

12 create waste and pollution

产生垃圾废料和污染

不要把这个短语里的 waste 理解成浪费 ✗

比较：

- drop litter in public places
  在公共场所乱丢废弃物

环　境

- household waste
  生活垃圾（名词短语）

- industrial waste
  工业废料（名词短语）

对比：

- reduce waste　减少垃圾

- recycle waste　循环利用废弃物

13 a throw-away culture

使用物品之后很快就丢弃、不重复使用或者循环利用的社会风气

对比：

- avoid single-use items　避免使用一次性的物品

- reuse shopping bags　重复使用购物袋

- fabric shopping bags　由织物制成的购物袋，这是目前英美环保组织最推荐使用的购物袋，要比 plastic shopping bags 更环保（more eco-friendly）

- recycle as much as possible
  尽可能地循环利用使用物品

- recycle cans and bottles　循环利用金属罐和瓶子

- recycle old household items
  循环利用已经老化的家庭用品

14 plastic packaging

（产品的）塑料外包装

- plastic containers　塑料的容器，例如：
  plastic bottles 和 plastic boxes

- do not break down easily　不会轻易地分解

对比：

- choose products with less packaging
  选择外包装更少的产品

- eco-friendly containers　环保的容器

15 raise public environmental awareness

提高公众的环境意识

- environmental education programmes in schools
  由学校提供的环境教育项目

- use double-sided printing
  （打印文件时）选用双面打印

- future generations　未来的人们

环　境

动植物

1 protect endangered species

保护濒危物种

extinction 是名词，extinct 是形容词

- face extinction　濒临灭绝

- become extinct / die out　灭绝

2 the illegal trade in ivory and rhino horns

对象牙和犀牛角的非法交易（名词短语）

- are hunted for their skins
  （老虎等）由于它们的兽皮而被捕猎（这个短语里的 skin 按习惯使用复数）

  are hunted for their meat, are hunted for their fur（皮大衣，毛皮），are hunted for their horns（角）等也都是野生动物被捕猎的常见原因

- fur coats　皮大衣，"皮草"

- whaling and sealing
  捕鲸和捕杀海豹的行为（名词短语）

- illegal wildlife products
  非法的野生生物制品（名词短语）

对比:
□ combat poaching （政府）打击偷猎行为

3 protect wildlife habitats
保护野生动植物的栖息地

□ human activities 人类的活动

□ cause climate change 导致气候变化

□ polar bears 北极熊

□ global warming 全球变暖

□ cause the polar ice caps to melt 导致极地冰盖融化

□ log forests 砍伐森林

□ cut down large numbers of trees 砍伐大量的树木

4 damage the ecosystem
破坏生态系统

□ disrupt food chains 扰乱食物链

□ threaten the food sources of wild animals
威胁野生动物的食物来源

□ reduce biodiversity 削弱生物的多样性

5 create more nature reserves
设立更多的自然保护区

□ create more wildlife reserves
建立更多的野生生物保护区

□ are interesting and educational
有趣并且很有知识性的

动植物

- help people to learn about wildlife
  帮助人们了解野生生物

- can roam, fly or swim freely
  （野生动物们）能自由地走动、飞翔或畅游

6 man-made habitat / artificial habitat
人造的动植物栖息地，例如动物园

- are kept in cages （动物们）被关在笼子里

- lose their freedom 失去自由

- feel lonely and frustrated 感到孤独而且情绪低落

- change their habits （动物们）改变它们的生活习性

- irresponsible zookeepers 不负责任的动物园管理员

对比：

- help to protect endangered species
  （动物园）有助于保护濒危的物种

- are interesting and educational 有趣而且很有知识性

- help children to learn about wild animals
  帮助儿童们了解野生动物

7 animal testing
动物试验

- animal experimentation 动物实验

- laboratory animals 在实验室里被使用的动物

- are kept in cages 被关在笼子里

- cause suffering to them　给它们造成痛苦

- is morally wrong
  从道德角度来看是错误的，是不道德的

- should be respected
  (动物的权利) 应该受到尊重

对比：

- animal rights groups　动物权益保护团体

- minimise their suffering　尽量减少它们的痛苦

- reliable alternatives　可靠的替代方法

- medical research　医学研究

- medical discoveries　医学发现

- develop new medicines and vaccines
  研发新的药品和疫苗

当表示不同种类的药物时，medicine 可以使用复数形式

- pharmaceutical companies　制药公司

- test the safety of new medicines
  检测新药物的安全性

动植物

议论文话题 *28*

犯 罪

1 **the increasing crime rates /**
the rising crime rates
上升的犯罪率（名词短语）

- □ break the law　违法
- □ commit a crime / commit crimes　犯罪

  native speakers 有时也直接把 crime 当作不可数名词使用，所以 commit crime 也是地道短语

- □ prevent crime　预防犯罪
- □ reduce crime rates　降低犯罪率

  比较：

- □ address the root causes of crime
  从根本上去解决犯罪问题
- □ create jobs　创造就业
- □ reduce poverty　减轻贫困
- □ reduce social inequality　减少社会不公正

2 **punish criminals**
惩罚罪犯

- □ serious offences　严重的罪行

226

- □ are sent to prison 被送进监狱

- □ serve prison sentences 在监狱里服刑

  它的意思不是指"被关进监狱罚背句子"

- □ lose their freedom 失去他们的自由

- □ cannot pose a threat to others
  不能再对别人构成威胁

- □ make them reflect on their actions
  让他们反思自己的行为

- □ deter crime 震慑犯罪

- □ deter criminals 震慑罪犯

对比:

- □ lead to prison overcrowding 导致监狱里面人满为患

- □ lead to resentment 导致怨恨的情绪

- □ may be wrongly convicted
  (有些人) 可能是被误判有罪的

3 are released from prison
被从监狱释放出来

- □ released prisoners / former prisoners 被释放的囚犯

- □ people with a criminal record 有犯罪记录的人

- □ are treated unfairly 受到不公正的待遇

- □ find it difficult to find a job 感到很难找工作

- □ do not have a steady source of income
  没有稳定的收入来源

犯罪

- lead to resentment 导致怨恨的情绪

- are likely to re-offend 很可能会再次犯罪

  【区分】offence 是名词，罪行；offender 也是名词，指违法者。re-offend 是动词，再次犯罪。而 offensive 则是形容词，指带有冒犯性的，例如一些电影里的 offensive language

4 reform criminals
改造罪犯

- provide counseling to them
  为他们提供心理方面的咨询

- provide them with vocational training
  为他们提供职业培训

- increase their employability 增强他们的就业适应性

- strong family support 来自于家人的坚定支持

- help them re-enter society 帮助他们重新走入社会

- reduce re-offending 减少再次犯罪的可能性

- reform them into contributing members of society
  把他们改造成能为社会做贡献的社会成员

- become law-abiding citizens 变成守法的公民

- obey the law 守法

对比：

- is not a sufficient punishment
  （某种措施）惩罚的力度不够

5 **minor crimes**
比较轻的罪行

【实例】vandalism 破坏公共财物, shoplifting 在商店里"顺手牵羊", driving without a license 无证驾驶等通常是被视为 minor crimes

□ pay fines　交纳罚款

□ community service　社区服务
（在英美，从事社区服务是对非暴力罪犯的最常见改造方式之一）

6 **media reports on crime**
媒体对犯罪进行的报导

□ focus on violent crime　集中地报导暴力犯罪

□ sensationalise crime　对犯罪进行过度渲染

□ attract more viewers, listeners or readers
吸引更多的观众、听众或读者

□ mislead the public　误导公众

□ increase people's fear of crime
进一步增强人们对犯罪的恐惧感

□ cause emotional suffering to the victims
给犯罪的受害者们造成心理伤害

7 **increase security measures**
增强安全防范措施

□ areas with high crime rates　犯罪高发区

犯　罪

- increase police patrol　增派警察巡逻

- install security cameras in public places
  在公共场所安装安全监控摄像头

- improve community safety　增进社区安全

对比:

- invade people's privacy　侵犯人们的隐私

- restrict people's freedom　限制人们的自由

- restrictive measures　让人们感到很受限制的措施

8 security cameras
安全监控摄像头

- public places　公共场所

- prevent crime　预防犯罪

- crime prevention　对于犯罪的预防

- deter crime　震慑犯罪

- deter criminals　震慑罪犯

- catch criminals / arrest criminals　抓捕罪犯

9 carry guns
携带枪支

【BBC 例句】Most front-line officers in the UK do not **carry guns**.

- police officers　警官

- protect the public　保护公众安全

- □ prevent crime
  预防犯罪

- □ deter crime
  震慑犯罪

- □ violent crimes
  暴力犯罪

- □ armed criminals
  持枪的罪犯（不要误解成"有胳膊的罪犯"）

- □ use guns in self-defence
  （警官）出于自卫而使用枪支

对比：

- □ may shoot innocent people　可能会伤及无辜

- □ alternatives to guns　枪支的替代手段

 英美 背景 pepper spray（胡椒喷雾器，名字听起来有点搞笑，其实威力挺大，并不只是"防狼工具"）和 Taser（电击枪）也都是英美警官们的常用武器

犯　罪

⊙ **Task 1 小作文里的** ◉
高频短语练习

请扫描二维码（scan the QR code），或者登录音频卡上面的网址，找到"小作文的高频短语翻译练习"这个文件，并在一张横格纸上写出您认为准确的答案。

* * *

当中国同学们在互联网上提到 IELTS 考试时，用得最多的表情符号就是两行眼泪的符号。但有一天突然要告别这个不仅虐身而且虐心的考试时，每个人却都有着太多的感触和感悟。也许，这种 love-hate relationship 就是 IELTS 考试的真正魅力所在。